British Blues Rock in Playlists Volume 1

Edited by Jesse Shanks

Introduction

The number of songs available on Apple Music is a constantly moving target, estimates ranging from 35 to 90 million. One of the major concerns users have is music discovery. Many argue that Spotify offers better discovery features compared to Apple Music. Personally, I believe that creating your own playlists is one of the best ways to discover music. The automatic suggestions of related songs that come from the music processing system can also aid in finding new music.

During my younger years, I frequently read Rolling Stone magazine and spent significant time going through record reviews, articles, and Random Notes. While they covered many musicians whose albums, cassettes, and later CDs I owned, they also introduced me to artists who never received much airplay or exposure on television. I hesitated to spend money on unfamiliar music.

Initially, I resisted subscribing to streaming services, primarily due to thriftiness. However, when I obtained an Apple One subscription, I gradually delved into it. At first, I created playlists as I had done in the past, reminiscent of the long-lost mixtape era. I would record individual songs from an LP onto a cassette, one by one, to compile a personalized selection of favorite music. However, these tapes often became monotonous after a while.

One year, I attended a MacWorld event where I encountered a stereo system connected to a hard drive containing hundreds of songs. It allowed for dynamic playlists that could be shuffled—a revelation.

Subsequently, SoundJam, iTunes, iPod, and other advancements followed. However, these were limited to the music files one physically possessed, whether purchased or obtained through other means. In retrospect, the cost of Apple Music outweighs the time spent downloading, copying, renaming, and organizing files.

Then came Apple Music, providing on-demand access to millions of songs. Not every song was available, of course, but it was a step closer to musical paradise. As mentioned earlier, I continued creating playlists consisting of 15 to 40 songs that I could play straight through or shuffle. One day, while exploring Eric Clapton's music and delving into Cream, I came across Ginger Baker, the drummer of that legendary band. I realized I had read about his post-Cream career in Rolling Stone but had hardly listened to any of it. Consequently, I compiled a playlist featuring a few songs from each of his albums. As I listened to this playlist (and thoroughly enjoyed it), I felt it was limited. I thought it might be better to create a playlist encompassing all his post-Cream albums and shuffle it. Break on through to the other side!

In this particular case, I discovered that I could listen to his entire catalog on shuffle and rarely hear the same playlist twice in any session. Moreover, occasionally, a lesser-known gem would emerge, akin to finding a piece of gold. I became a music miner.

Certain artists cannot be contained within a single playlist, prompting me to create multiple playlists for some careers. Various thematic or conceptual playlist ideas can be formulated, but that discussion is better suited for another time. During my teenage years, I cherished a two-disc set titled "History of Eric Clapton," which showcased cuts from the guitar virtuoso's career from the early Sixties to the mid-Seventies. This album significantly impacted my music fandom as it introduced me to The Yardbirds, King Curtis, Delaney & Bonnie, Derek & the Dominos, and more. Therefore, I decided to recreate this album in a playlist. The outcome was reasonably satisfying, but I realized it would be better to create a playlist for each phase of Clapton's career. This way, the songs would flow harmoniously without the jarring transition from "Smokestack Lightnin'" to "Forever Man." Ultimately, I divided Clapton's career into eight separate playlists, comprising over 600 songs in total. Each playlist stands well on its own while also being able to combine into even larger playlists.

Thus, a fantastic hobby is born for music enthusiasts.

British Blues Rock in Playlists Volume 1

For some reason, I don't exactly how the blues, and particularly British Blues Rock, became part of my life. As mentioned in the introduction, the History of Eric Clapton album was a landmark purchase. I have always enjoyed Deep Purple as an entertaining, hard-rocking band. I will freely admit that they don't exactly fit comfortably in the blues-rock category, but they certainly emerged from the same primoridial musical swamp that yielded so many in the broad category headed by the holy trinity of Eric Clapton, Jeff Beck, and Jimmy Page. The Purple Canon here is guided by the lineup changes. There are the earliest recordings in Purple 1 with Ritchie Blackmore, Jon Lord, Nick Simper, Ian Paice, and Rod Evans in the group to make up the first playlist with an interesting look at their efforts to distinguish themselves. Then Purple 2 features the indelible lineup of Ritchie Blackmore, Jon Lord, Ian Paice, Ian Gillian, and Roger Glover.

It is a personal aggravation that I never saw a group named "Deep Purple" take the stage. I went to see Ritchie Blackmore with Rainbow on their "Difficult to Cure" tour with Roger Glover and Joe Lynn Turner. Ian Gillian's band was in a festival I saw at the Loreley Amphitheater in Germany. I also caught Whitesnake in Frankfurt, Germany with David Coverdale, Ian Paice, and Jon Lord. This was during a time when the band members were not getting along. They would re-unite in 1984 and those cuts are on this playlist.

Purple 3 covers the short period back in 1973-1975 when David Coverdale fronted the band for two of their most famous albums. They also performed at a televised concert called California Jam which made a huge impression on me as a youngster. Ritchie Blackmore left the band after that and Tommy Bolin came in. Much ink was spilled in rock magazines over this change, right up until Tommy Bolin left the band and died soon after. The playlist Bolin allows the examination of the talented, mercurial guitarist with the band and solo. This led to the aforementioned hiatus from 1976-1984 that pretty much killed the band's legacy as a seminal part of "hard rock" during a time when hard rock music exploded and the band members continues in the various entities.

Purple 4 is a mix of band configurations from 1976 to their most recent recordings in 2021 with and without Ritchie Blackmore. Legendary guitarist Steve Morse takes a fascinating turn with the band. The Playlist Other Purples is a mix of recordings in which members of the band are featured or were a driving force. This is a very good listen on shuffle play to hear the various experiments mixed with the Purple style and sound.

Status Quo is another blues-rock band that has been around for a long time. They came up as a psychedelic band in the Sixties with "Pictures of Matchstick Men" one of those songs that shows up on many lists that include "Crimson & Clover", "In-A-Gadda-Da-Vida," and other relics of the trippy years. The playlist Status Quo 1 explores that time with expanded editions of their first two albums and a couple of compilations, one being a complete collection of their recordings with their first label in "The Complete Pye

Collection" and "The Technicolor Dreams Of The Status Quo: The Complete 60s Recordings," which includes some of their earliest recordings as The Spectres and Traffic Jam. But the transition from this era to what they became is found here as well.

Many would be surprised to find out that Status is one of the most successful groups of all time in the UK. Status Quo 2 collects many of their studio albums, although Apple does not have them all by any stretch. The group essays a broad range of material from English folk to psychedelia to blues and Beatlesque pop. Status Quo amasses a marvelous collection of 164 live recordings including the group opening the Live Aid charity event at Wembley Stadium in July 1985.

Ten Years After, Alvin Lee, guitar, Leo Lyons, bass, Ric Lee, drums, and Chick Churchill on keyboards. has had career highlights such as being one of the memorable performances from the Woodstock movie to several memorable hit songs and successful album releases. TYA 1 captures those early years with their recordings with their original label. Only a recording of their memorable performance of "I'm Going Home" is on Apple Music from Woodstock. TYA 2 contains their material with their new label and their greatest commercial success, including live and studio. Also included is the material from their reunion. The group broke up in 1974 when superstar guitarist Alvin Lee went on his own with Ten Years Later.

The original group reunited in 1983 and recorded one studio album until 2003 when Lee left for good and was replaced by Joe Gooch. Lee mostly played and recorded under his own name following his split from the band. He died from complications during a routine medical procedure on 6 March 2013. This later iteration of Ten Years After has released several albums, both live and studio, and most recently Gooch and original member Leo Lyons left to be replaced by veteran bass player Colin Hodgkinson and singer/guitarist Marcus Bonfanti. TYA 3 documents the recordings of the Alvin Lee-less Ten Years After. A final playlist called "Alvin Lee" is made up of his solo career outside of the band he founded and fronted for so many years. Both studio and live recordings present the man called The Fast Guitar in the West.

Of course, these are just my personal choices. As the curator of your own playlists, you can make different decisions based on your preferences and the artists you're working with. This is another advantage of Apple Music—it allows for customization. Each playlist is a work in progress and can be modified at any time. There have been instances where a song didn't fit despite belonging to the same era. It can be enjoyable to discover more obscure tracks to add to a playlist, representing different phases of an artist's career. Compilations of an artist's work can unveil interesting songs that were previously unreleased and can be incorporated into specific playlists. Additionally, guest appearances by an artist on another musician's record can make a delightful addition. Some of these songs are readily available among the top tracks, while others require a search or a fortunate encounter on another occasion.

Each playlist has is a QR code to take you to that particular playlist in the Apple Music system. That is an interesting community feature that is far from being completely developed. You can find and follow other users, to see what their playlists are, and what they are listening to, if authorized.

Deep Purple

Deep Purple, one of the most influential and enduring rock bands in history, emerged from the depths of the late 1960s music scene, leaving an indelible mark on the genre. With their virtuosic musicianship, powerful stage presence, and boundary-pushing sound, Deep Purple became pioneers of hard rock, captivating audiences around the world. Let's dive into the captivating biography of this legendary band.

Deep Purple was formed in Hertford, England, in 1968. The initial lineup consisted of guitarist Ritchie Blackmore, keyboardist Jon Lord, bassist Nick Simper, drummer Ian Paice, and vocalist Rod Evans. With their debut album, "Shades of Deep Purple" (1968), the band quickly established their unique blend of psychedelic and progressive rock, earning them a devoted fan base.

Deep Purple's sophomore album, "The Book of Taliesyn" (1968), showcased their evolving sound, incorporating classical influences and ambitious compositions. However, it was their breakthrough third album, simply titled "Deep Purple" (1969), that propelled them to international fame. With iconic tracks like "Hush" and "Kentucky Woman," the album solidified their status as a force to be reckoned with in the rock world.

In 1969, Deep Purple underwent a significant lineup change that would define their most successful era. Vocalist Ian Gillan and bassist Roger Glover replaced Rod Evans and Nick Simper, respectively, joining forces with Blackmore, Lord, and Paice. This new lineup, known as Mark II, released the seminal album "Deep Purple in Rock" (1970), unleashing a heavier, more intense sound that set the template for hard rock.

With subsequent albums like "Fireball" (1971) and "Machine Head" (1972), Deep Purple achieved unparalleled success. "Machine Head" spawned their most iconic song, "Smoke on the Water," an anthem that resonated with audiences worldwide. The band's dynamic chemistry, highlighted by Blackmore's searing guitar solos, Lord's intricate keyboard work, Gillan's soaring vocals, Glover's solid basslines, and

Paice's thunderous drumming, propelled them to the pinnacle of rock stardom.

As the '70s progressed, Deep Purple continued to evolve their sound, incorporating elements of funk, soul, and progressive rock. Albums like "Who Do We Think We Are" (1973) and "Burn" (1974) showcased the band's musical versatility, but internal tensions led to the departure of Gillan and Glover, marking the end of the Mark II era.

Deep Purple underwent multiple lineup changes in the following years, embracing new vocalists and guitarists such as David Coverdale, Glenn Hughes, and Tommy Bolin. While these transitional periods produced albums like "Come Taste the Band" (1975) and "Stormbringer" (1974), they faced challenges amid shifting musical landscapes and personal struggles.

Deep Purple experienced several reunions and lineup adjustments throughout the '80s, '90s, and beyond. The classic Mark II lineup reunited in 1984, releasing albums like "Perfect Strangers" (1984) and "The House of Blue Light" (1987). The band's resilience and dedication to their craft allowed them to maintain their status as a powerhouse in the hard rock scene, influencing countless bands and generations of musicians.

Deep Purple's impact on rock music cannot be overstated. Their groundbreaking fusion of hard rock, progressive elements, and virtuoso performances set the stage for future generations of musicians. Their distinctive sound, characterized by thunderous riffs, intricate arrangements, and unforgettable anthems, continues to inspire and resonate with fans worldwide.

Deep Purple's unwavering passion and unrelenting drive to push musical boundaries solidified their place in rock history. From their early days as pioneers of hard rock to their enduring legacy as one of the genre's most influential bands, Deep Purple's music continues to captivate and inspire audiences across the globe. Their journey stands as a testament to the power of rock 'n' roll and the enduring spirit of these legendary musicians.

Playlist: Purple 1

Deep Purple is a legendary rock group that emerged in the late 1960s, leaving an indelible mark on the music scene with their electrifying performances and groundbreaking sound. Comprising Ritchie Blackmore, Jon Lord, Nick Simper, Ian Paice, and Rod Evans, this lineup showcased the band's early brilliance. Let's delve into the albums that defined their formative years: "Shades of Deep Purple" , "The Book of Taliesyn" , and "Deep Purple" .

"Shades of Deep Purple" :
Released in 1968, "Shades of Deep Purple" introduced the world to the unique blend of rock, blues, and progressive elements that would become the band's signature style. With mesmerizing tracks like "Hush" and "Mandrake Root," the album showcased the virtuosic guitar work of Ritchie Blackmore and the captivating keyboards of Jon Lord. The Deluxe Edition treats listeners to rare demos and previously unreleased material, offering a deeper glimpse into the band's early creative process.

"The Book of Taliesyn" :
Following the success of their debut, Deep Purple unleashed "The Book of Taliesyn" in 1968. This album further expanded their musical horizons, weaving together dynamic rock compositions with nods to classical influences. Standout tracks such as "Wring That Neck" and their mesmerizing cover of Neil Diamond's "Kentucky Woman" demonstrated the band's versatility and penchant for experimentation. The Deluxe Edition presents alternate versions and studio outtakes, providing fans with a fascinating glimpse into the band's evolution.

"Deep Purple" :
Released in 1969, the self-titled "Deep Purple" marked a pivotal moment for the band as they honed their signature sound. This album showcased the explosive chemistry between Blackmore's searing guitar riffs, Lord's atmospheric keyboards, Simper's driving basslines, Paice's thunderous drums, and Evans' captivating vocals. From the anthemic

"Hallelujah" to the brooding "April," the album displayed the band's ability to deliver both high-octane rockers and introspective ballads. The Deluxe Edition includes bonus tracks and rare live recordings, capturing the band's energy in a live setting.

As the band's early albums continue to resonate with fans, they provide a glimpse into the foundation upon which Deep Purple built their enduring legacy. These Deluxe Editions offer a treasure trove of additional material, allowing fans to immerse themselves in the band's creative process and witness their growth as musicians.

Deep Purple's early years with Ritchie Blackmore, Jon Lord, Nick Simper, Ian Paice, and Rod Evans were a crucial chapter in the evolution of rock music. Their bold experimentation, virtuosity, and captivating performances laid the groundwork for the band's future triumphs. Whether you're a longtime fan or discovering their music for the first time, these albums are a testament to the soulful depths of Deep Purple and their enduring impact on the rock 'n' roll landscape.

- And the Address   4:38   Shades of Deep Purple
- Hush   4:24   Class of '68
- One More Rainy Day   3:39   Shades of Deep Purple
- Prelude: Happiness / I'm So Glad   7:19   Shades of Deep Purple
- Mandrake Root   6:09   Shades of Deep Purple
- Help!   6:01   Shades of Deep Purple
- Love Help Me   3:49   Shades of Deep Purple

- Hey Joe   7:33   Shades of Deep Purple
- Shadows (Album Outtake) 3:38   Shades of Deep Purple
- Love Help Me (Instrumental)   3:29   Shades of Deep Purple
- Help! (Alternate Take)   5:23   Shades of Deep Purple
- Hey Joe (BBC Top Gear Session, 01/14/69) 4:05   Shades of Deep Purple
- Hush (Live US TV, 1968)   3:53   Shades of Deep Purple
- Listen, Learn, Read On   4:04   The Book of Taliesyn
- Kentucky Woman   4:44   The Book of Taliesyn
- Exposition / We Can Work It Out 7:07   The Book of Taliesyn
- Shield   6:06   The Book of Taliesyn
- Anthem   6:31   The Book of Taliesyn
- River Deep, Mountain High   10:12   The Book of Taliesyn
- Oh No No No (Studio Outtake, 12/68)   4:25   The Book of Taliesyn
- It's All Over (BBC Top Gear Session, 01/14/69)   4:14   The Book of Taliesyn
- Hey Bop a Re Bop (BBC Top Gear Session, 01/14/69) 3:31 The Book of Taliesyn
- Wring That Neck (BBC Top Gear Session, 01/14/69) 4:42 The Book of Taliesyn
- Playground (Remixed Instrumental Studio Outtake, 08/18/68)   4:29   The Book of Taliesyn
- Chasing Shadows   5:34   Deep Purple
- Blind   5:26   Deep Purple

- Lalena   5:05   Deep Purple
- Fault Line   1:46   Deep Purple
- The Painter 3:51   Deep Purple
- Why Didn't Rosemary?   5:04   Deep Purple
- Bird Has Flown   5:36   Deep Purple
- April   12:10   Deep Purple
- Bird Has Flown (Alternate A-Side Version) 2:54   Deep Purple
- Emmaretta (Studio B-Side) 3:00   Deep Purple
- Emmaretta (BBC Top Gear Session, 01/14/69)   3:09 Deep Purple
- Lalena (BBC Radio Session, 06/24/69)   3:33   Deep Purple
- The Painter (BBC Radio Session, 06/24/69)   2:18 Deep Purple

Playlist: Purple 2

Deep Purple's mid-career phase witnessed the band's enduring resilience and evolution that solidified their status as one of rock music's most formidable forces. With a lineup featuring Ritchie Blackmore, Jon Lord, Ian Paice, Ian Gillan, and Roger Glover, the band released a series of iconic albums that pushed the boundaries of their sound and captivated audiences worldwide. Let's embark on a journey through the sonic landscape of Deep Purple, from "Concerto for Group and Orchestra" (Live) to "The Battle Rages On..."

"Concerto for Group and Orchestra" (Live):
Recorded in 1969, this groundbreaking live album showcased Deep Purple's fusion of rock music and classical elements. Collaborating with the Royal Philharmonic Orchestra, the band created a grandiose and immersive musical experience. The album highlighted the band's technical prowess and experimental spirit, setting the stage for their subsequent sonic exploration.

"Deep Purple In Rock":
Released in 1970, "Deep Purple In Rock" marked a turning point for the band as they delved deeper into the realms of hard rock and heavy metal. Songs like "Speed King" and "Child in Time" demonstrated the band's raw power, while tracks like "Black Night" became timeless anthems. The album solidified Deep Purple's reputation as masters of the genre, blazing a trail for generations of rockers to follow.

"Fireball":
Following the success of "Deep Purple In Rock," the band continued their ascent with "Fireball" in 1971. This album showcased a more diverse range of musical influences,

combining heavy rock with elements of blues and progressive rock. Tracks like "Strange Kind of Woman" and the title track demonstrated the band's ability to create infectious hooks while maintaining their signature intensity.

"Machine Head":
Arguably their most influential and iconic release, "Machine Head" (1972) remains a cornerstone of Deep Purple's discography. This album birthed timeless classics such as "Smoke on the Water" and "Highway Star," which cemented the band's place in rock history. With its impeccable songwriting, blistering guitar solos, and unmatched energy, "Machine Head" propelled Deep Purple into global stardom.

"Who Do We Think We Are":
Released in 1973, this album showcased Deep Purple's unrelenting passion and drive. Although tensions within the band were rising, they channeled their creative energy into tracks like "Woman from Tokyo" and "Rat Bat Blue." The Deluxe Edition offers bonus tracks that provide further insight into the band's artistic vision during this period.

"Made In Japan" [Live]:
Capturing Deep Purple's electrifying live performances, "Made In Japan" (1972) remains one of the greatest live albums of all time. The Deluxe Edition features additional tracks, offering a complete snapshot of the band's immense stage presence and improvisational prowess.

"Perfect Strangers" (Bonus Track Version):
After an extended hiatus, Deep Purple reunited in 1984 with "Perfect Strangers," marking a triumphant return to form.

The album's title track became an instant hit, showcasing the band's renewed chemistry and revitalized sound.

"The House of Blue Light":
Released in 1987, this album continued to showcase Deep Purple's ability to craft hard-hitting rock anthems. Tracks like "Bad Attitude" and "Call of the Wild" solidified their place in the '80s rock scene, proving that the band's fire still burned brightly.

"Nobody's Perfect" (Live):
Capturing the band's raw energy on stage, "Nobody's Perfect" (1988) showcased Deep Purple's live prowess during their reinvigorated phase. With blistering renditions of classics like "Highway Star" and "Smoke on the Water," the album exemplified the band's enduring legacy as a captivating live act.

"The Battle Rages On...":
Released in 1993, this album marked the final studio collaboration between Blackmore and Deep Purple. Despite the internal conflicts, the band delivered a collection of powerful tracks, including the title track and "Anya," demonstrating their unwavering commitment to their craft.

Deep Purple's mid-career phase represents a testament to their resilience, musical growth, and unwavering commitment to rock 'n' roll. From the experimental fusion of classical and rock to their mastery of hard-hitting anthems, these albums stand as a testament to the band's enduring legacy. With each release, Deep Purple etched their name in the annals of rock history, leaving behind a sonic legacy that continues to inspire and captivate audiences to this day.

- Hallelujah   3:40   A Fire In the Sky: A Career-Spanning Collection
- Concerto for Group and Orchestra, First Movement: Moderato — Allegro (Live) 19:11   Concerto for Group and Orchestra (Live)
- Concerto for Group and Orchestra, Second Movement: Andante Part 1 (Live)   6:33   Concerto for Group and Orchestra (Live)
- Concerto for Group and Orchestra, Second Movement: Andante Conclusion (Live) 12:27   Concerto for Group and Orchestra (Live)
- Concerto for Group and Orchestra, Third Movement: Vivace — Presto (Live)   15:31   Concerto for Group and Orchestra (Live)
- Speed King 5:55   Deep Purple In Rock
- Bloodsucker 4:15   Deep Purple In Rock
- Child In Time   10:19   Deep Purple In Rock
- Flight of the Rat   7:57   Deep Purple In Rock
- Into the Fire   3:29   Deep Purple In Rock
- Living Wreck   4:35   Deep Purple In Rock
- Hard Lovin' Man   7:13   Deep Purple In Rock
- Black Night (Single Version)   3:27   Deepest Purple: The Very Best of Deep Purple (30th Anniversary Edition)
- Fireball   3:25   Fireball
- No No No 6:53   Fireball

- Demon's Eye   5:21   Fireball
- Anyone's Daughter 4:44   Fireball
- The Mule   5:21   Fireball
- Fools   8:18   Fireball
- No One Came   6:29   Fireball
- Strange Kind of Woman   3:52   The Very Best of Deep
  Purple
- Highway Star   6:06   Machine Head
- Maybe I'm a Leo   4:50   Machine Head
- Pictures of Home   5:03   Machine Head
- Never Before   3:58   Machine Head
- Smoke On the Water   5:40   Machine Head
- Lazy7:22   Machine Head
- Space Truckin'   4:32   Machine Head
- Woman from Tokyo   5:49   Who Do We Think
  We Are
- Mary Long 4:26   Who Do We Think We Are
- Super Trouper   2:55   Who Do We Think We Are
- Smooth Dancer   4:11   Who Do We Think We Are
- Rat Bat Blue5:26   Who Do We Think We Are
- Place In Line   6:33   Who Do We Think We Are
- Our Lady   5:10   Who Do We Think We Are
- Woman from Tokyo ('99 Remix Version) 6:42   Who
  Do We Think We Are
- Woman from Tokyo (Alternate Bridge Version)   1:26
  Who Do We Think We Are
- Painted Horse (Studio Outtake)   5:21   Who Do We
  Think We Are

- Our Lady ('99 Remix Version)   6:06   Who Do We Think We Are
- Rat Bat Blue (Writing Session)   0:56   Who Do We Think We Are
- Rat Bat Blue ('99 Remix Version) 5:47   Who Do We Think We Are
- First Day Jam (Instrumental)   11:28   Who Do We Think We Are
- Highway Star (Live)6:41   Made In Japan [Live]
- Child In Time (Live)   12:33   Made In Japan [Live]
- Smoke On the Water (Live)7:18   Made In Japan [Live]
- The Mule (Live)   9:28   Made In Japan [Live]
- Strange Kind of Woman (Live)   9:52   Made In Japan [Live]
- Lazy (Live) 10:24   Made In Japan [Live]
- Space Truckin' (Live)   19:49   Made In Japan [Live]
- Black Night (Live In Osaka, JP, 08/15/72) 6:58   Made In Japan [Live]
- Speed King (Live In Osaka, JP, 08/15/72) 8:28   Made In Japan [Live]
- Black Night (Live In Osaka, JP, 08/16/72) 6:58   Made In Japan [Live]
- Lucille (Live In Osaka, JP, 08/16/72)   9:03   Made In Japan [Live]
- Black Night (Live In Tokyo, JP, 08/17/72) 8:01   Made In Japan [Live]
- Speed King (Live In Tokyo, JP, 08/17/72) 7:19   Made In Japan [Live]

- Knocking at Your Back Door   7:05   Perfect Strangers (Bonus Track Version)
- Under the Gun   4:38   Perfect Strangers (Bonus Track Version)
- Nobody's Home   4:00   Perfect Strangers (Bonus Track Version)
- Mean Streak   4:22   Perfect Strangers (Bonus Track Version)
- Perfect Strangers   5:28   Perfect Strangers (Bonus Track Version)
- A Gypsy's Kiss   5:12   Perfect Strangers (Bonus Track Version)
- Wasted Sunsets   3:55   Perfect Strangers (Bonus Track Version)
- Hungry Daze   4:58   Perfect Strangers (Bonus Track Version)
- Not Responsible   4:47   Perfect Strangers (Bonus Track Version)
- Son of Alerik   10:02   Perfect Strangers (Bonus Track Version)
- Bad Attitude   4:46   The House of Blue Light
- The Unwritten Law 4:37   The House of Blue Light
- Call of the Wild   4:53   The House of Blue Light
- Mad Dog   4:34   The House of Blue Light
- Black & White   3:42   The House of Blue Light
- Hard Lovin' Woman   3:25   The House of Blue Light
- The Spanish Archer 4:59   The House of Blue Light

- Strangeways 5:58   The House of Blue Light
- Mitzi Dupree   5:05   The House of Blue Light
- Dead or Alive   4:42   The House of Blue Light
- Highway Star (Live) 6:10   Nobody's Perfect (Live)
- Strange Kind of Woman (Live)   7:35   Nobody's Perfect (Live)
- Dead or Alive (Live)   7:05   Nobody's Perfect (Live)
- Perfect Strangers (Live)   6:24   Nobody's Perfect (Live)
- Hard Lovin' Woman (Live) 5:04   Nobody's Perfect (Live)
- Bad Attitude (Live) 5:30   Nobody's Perfect (Live)
- Knocking at Your Back Door (Live) 11:24   Nobody's Perfect (Live)
- Child In Time (Live)   10:36   Nobody's Perfect (Live)
- Lazy (Live) 5:10   Nobody's Perfect (Live)
- Space Truckin' (Live)   6:02   Nobody's Perfect (Live)
- Black Night (Live) 6:07   Nobody's Perfect (Live)
- Woman from Tokyo (Live) 3:59   Nobody's Perfect (Live)
- Smoke On the Water (Live) 7:43   Nobody's Perfect (Live)
- Hush (1988 Studio Version) 3:32   Nobody's Perfect (Live)
- The Battle Rages On   5:55   The Battle Rages On...

- Lick It Up 3:59 The Battle Rages On...
- Anya 6:31 The Battle Rages On...
- Talk About Love 4:06 The Battle Rages On...
- Time to Kill 5:48 The Battle Rages On...
- Ramshackle Man 5:33 The Battle Rages On...
- A Twist In the Tale 4:15 The Battle Rages On...
- Nasty Piece of Work 4:35 The Battle Rages On...
- Solitaire 4:41 The Battle Rages On...
- One Man's Meat 4:38 The Battle Rages On...

Playlist: Purple 3

After a significant lineup change, Deep Purple entered a new era in the early 1970s, infusing their sound with fresh energy and unleashing a wave of rock powerhouses. With Ritchie Blackmore, Ian Paice, Jon Lord, Glenn Hughes, and David Coverdale at the helm, the band released a series of albums that showcased their creative prowess and unrelenting passion for rock music. Let's dive into the sonic landscape of

Deep Purple during this era, highlighting albums like "Burn," "In Concert '72 (2012 Mix)," and "The Official Deep Purple (Overseas) Live Series: Paris 1975."

"Burn":
Released in 1974, "Burn" marked the debut of Deep Purple's revitalized lineup. The album exuded a renewed sense of urgency and musical exploration, with Blackmore's incendiary guitar work, Lord's masterful keyboards, and the dynamic vocal interplay between Hughes and Coverdale. Tracks like the title track, "Mistreated," and "You Fool No One" showcased the band's ability to fuse hard rock with elements of funk and soul, creating a sound that was uniquely their own.

"In Concert '72 (2012 Mix)":
This live album, released in 2012, captures Deep Purple at the height of their powers during their 1972 tour. The 2012 mix brings a fresh perspective to the band's electrifying live performances, featuring standout renditions of classics such as "Highway Star" and "Space Truckin'." The album serves as a testament to the band's unparalleled stage presence and the immense energy they brought to their live shows.

"The Official Deep Purple (Overseas) Live Series: Paris 1975":
This live recording from 1975 immortalizes Deep Purple's explosive performance in Paris. With their trademark intensity and virtuosity on full display, the band delivers powerful renditions of tracks like "Burn," "Stormbringer," and "Mistreated." The album captures the band in their element, showcasing their ability to captivate audiences with their dynamic musicianship and commanding stage presence.

During this phase of their career, Deep Purple proved that change could lead to artistic rebirth. With the addition of Hughes and Coverdale, the band's sound embraced elements of funk, soul, and blues, while retaining their hard rock foundation. The chemistry between the band members was palpable, resulting in albums that pushed boundaries and left an indelible impact on the rock music landscape.

Deep Purple's music during this era was characterized by blistering guitar solos, thunderous rhythms, soulful vocals, and a sense of unbridled energy. The albums "Burn," "In Concert '72 (2012 Mix)," and "The Official Deep Purple (Overseas) Live Series: Paris 1975" stand as testaments to the band's resilience, musicianship, and their ability to continually reinvent themselves.

Deep Purple's legacy during this period is one of explosive creativity, sonic innovation, and a relentless commitment to pushing the boundaries of rock music. These albums represent a crucial chapter in the band's storied career, leaving an enduring imprint on the hearts of fans and solidifying their place among the greatest rock acts of all time.

- Burn   6:04   Burn
- Might Just Take Your Life   4:40   Burn
- Lay Down, Stay Down   4:20   Burn
- Sail Away   5:53   Burn
- You Fool No One   4:48   Burn
- What's Goin' On Here   4:58   Burn

- Mistreated 7:29   Burn
- "A" 200   4:10   Burn
- Stormbringer   4:05   Stormbringer
- Love Don't Mean a Thing 4:23   Stormbringer
- Holy Man   4:30   Stormbringer
- Hold On   5:07   Stormbringer
- Lady Double Dealer 3:21   Stormbringer
- You Can't Do It Right   3:25   Stormbringer
- High Ball Shooter 4:28   Stormbringer
- The Gypsy 4:06   Stormbringer
- Soldier of Fortune 3:16   Stormbringer
- Introduction (Live at the Paris Theatre, London, 03/09/72) [2012 Mix]   0:15   In Concert '72 (2012 Mix)
- Highway Star (Live at the Paris Theatre, London, 03/09/72) [2012 Mix]   7:41   In Concert '72 (2012 Mix)
- Strange Kind of Woman (Live at the Paris Theatre, London, 03/09/72) [2012 Mix]   9:32   In Concert '72 (2012 Mix)
- Maybe I'm a Leo (Live at the Paris Theatre, London, 03/09/72) [2012 Mix]   5:35   In Concert '72 (2012 Mix)
- Smoke On the Water (Live at the Paris Theatre, London, 03/09/72) [2012 Mix]   7:31   In Concert '72 (2012 Mix)

- Never Before (Live at the Paris Theatre, London, 03/09/72) [2012 Mix]   5:18   In Concert '72 (2012 Mix)
- Lazy (Live at the Paris Theatre, London, 03/09/72) [2012 Mix]   9:22   In Concert '72 (2012 Mix)
- Space Truckin' (Live at the Paris Theatre, London, 03/09/72) [2012 Mix]   22:11   In Concert '72 (2012 Mix)
- Lucille (Live at the Paris Theatre, London, 03/09/72) [2012 Mix]   7:35   In Concert '72 (2012 Mix)
- Maybe I'm a Leo (Sound Check) [2012 Mix]   4:32   In Concert '72 (2012 Mix)
- Burn (Live in Paris 1975)   8:36   The Official Deep Purple (Overseas) Live Series: Paris 1975
- Stormbringer (Live in Paris 1975)   5:14   The Official Deep Purple (Overseas) Live Series: Paris 1975
- The Gypsy (Live in Paris 1975)   6:08   The Official Deep Purple (Overseas) Live Series: Paris 1975
- Lady Double Dealer (Live in Paris 1975)   4:25   The Official Deep Purple (Overseas) Live Series: Paris 1975
- Mistreated (Live in Paris 1975)   12:57   The Official Deep Purple (Overseas) Live Series: Paris 1975
- Smoke on the Water (Live in Paris 1975)   10:23   The Official Deep Purple (Overseas) Live Series: Paris 1975
- You Fool No One (Live in Paris 1975)   19:26   The Official Deep Purple (Overseas) Live Series: Paris 1975
- Space Truckin' (Live in Paris 1975)   21:23   The Official Deep Purple (Overseas) Live Series: Paris 1975

- Going Down (Live in Paris 1975) 5:16 The Official Deep Purple (Overseas) Live Series: Paris 1975
- Highway Star (Live in Paris 1975) 11:31 The Official Deep Purple (Overseas) Live Series: Paris 1975
- Interview with David Coverdale, Glenn Hughes, & Ian Paice (Bonus Track) 23:19 The Official Deep Purple (Overseas) Live Series: Paris 1975

Playlist: Purple 4

Deep Purple's storied career has been marked by a series of lineup changes, each bringing a unique flavor to the band's sound and creative direction. From the experimental years of Tommy Bolin to the enduring tenure of Steve Morse, Deep Purple continued to push boundaries and captivate audiences with their evolving lineup. Let's explore the albums and lineups that defined these distinct phases:

"Come Taste the Band":
1975-76: Jon Lord, Ian Paice, David Coverdale, Glenn Hughes & Tommy Bolin - Released in 1975, "Come Taste the Band" showcased the band's exploration of funk and soul influences, driven by Bolin's versatile guitar work and the captivating vocal interplay between Coverdale and Hughes. The album revealed a new sonic dimension for Deep Purple, embracing a more groove-oriented sound.

"Slaves and Masters" (Bonus Track Version):
1989-1992: Ritchie Blackmore, Jon Lord, Ian Paice, Roger Glover & Joe Lynn Turner This album, released in 1990, marked the return of Joe Lynn Turner as the band's vocalist. The record carried a melodic hard rock sound, featuring tracks like "King of Dreams" and "Love Conquers All." It showcased Deep Purple's ability to adapt to changing musical landscapes while maintaining their distinct musical identity.

"Purpendicular":
1994-2002: Ian Gillian, Roger Glover, Jon Lord, Ian Paice & Steve Morse Released in 1996, "Purpendicular" saw the introduction of guitarist Steve Morse. The album rejuvenated Deep Purple's sound with a fresh infusion of energy, featuring tracks like "Vavoom: Ted the Mechanic" and "Sometimes I Feel Like Screaming." It highlighted the band's enduring spirit and songwriting prowess.

"Rapture of the Deep":
2002-2021: Ian Paice, Roger Glover, Ian Gillian, Steve Morse & Don Airey Released in 2005, "Rapture of the Deep" showcased the band's continued musical maturity and versatility. With tracks like "Wrong Man" and "Rapture of

the Deep," Deep Purple demonstrated their ability to craft dynamic and powerful compositions, driven by Morse's intricate guitar work and Airey's keyboard wizardry.

"Now What?!" and "Infinite" (Bonus Track Version):
These albums, released in 2013 and 2017 respectively, solidified Deep Purple's status as enduring rock icons. The albums featured a blend of hard-hitting rock anthems and introspective ballads, with tracks like "Vincent Price" and "Time for Bedlam" displaying the band's unwavering commitment to their craft.

"Whoosh!":
Released in 2020, "Whoosh!" proved that Deep Purple's creative flame continued to burn brightly. The album showcased their trademark sound while incorporating modern elements, demonstrating their ability to stay relevant while retaining their classic rock essence.

In addition to these studio albums, Deep Purple's live recordings during these phases also captured the band's raw energy and captivating stage presence. Releases such as "In Concert With The London Symphony Orchestra (Live)," "Live In Newcastle 2001," and "The Infinite Live Recordings, Vol. 1" exemplified their electrifying live performances and showcased their enduring legacy as a formidable live act. Deep Purple's journey through lineup changes is a testament to their adaptability and unwavering passion for rock music. Each era brought a unique flavor to their sound, ensuring their relevance and impact over several decades. Through the changing tides, Deep Purple continued to push boundaries, captivate audiences, and solidify their place in the pantheon of rock legends.

- Comin' Home   3:56   Come Taste the Band
- Lady Luck   2:47   Come Taste the Band
- Gettin' Tighter   3:38   Come Taste the Band
- Dealer   3:50   Come Taste the Band
- I Need Love 4:23   Come Taste the Band
- Drifter   4:02   Come Taste the Band
- Love Child 3:08   Come Taste the Band
- This Time Around / Owed to 'G'   6:10   Come Taste the Band
- You Keep On Moving   5:22   Come Taste the Band
- King of Dreams   5:26   Slaves and Masters (Bonus Track Version)
- The Cut Runs Deep 5:37   Slaves and Masters (Bonus Track Version)
- Fire In the Basement   4:42   Slaves and Masters (Bonus Track Version)
- Truth Hurts 5:12   Slaves and Masters (Bonus Track Version)
- Breakfast In Bed   5:15   Slaves and Masters (Bonus Track Version)
- Love Conquers All 3:44   Slaves and Masters (Bonus Track Version)
- Fortuneteller   5:48   Slaves and Masters (Bonus Track Version)
- Too Much Is Not Enough   4:15   Slaves and Masters (Bonus Track Version)

- Wicked Ways   6:33   Slaves and Masters (Bonus Track Version)
- Slow Down Sister   5:57   Slaves and Masters (Bonus Track Version)
- Love Conquers All (Edit)   3:23   Slaves and Masters (Bonus Track Version)
- Vavoom: Ted the Mechanic 4:16   Purpendicular
- Loosen My Strings 5:56   Purpendicular
- Soon Forgotten   4:47   Purpendicular
- Sometimes I Feel Like Screaming   7:29   Purpendicular
- Cascades: I'm Not Your Lover   4:42   Purpendicular
- The Aviator 5:19   Purpendicular
- Rosa's Cantina   5:08   Purpendicular
- A Castle Full of Rascals   5:09   Purpendicular
- A Touch Away   4:36   Purpendicular
- Hey Cisco 5:53   Purpendicular
- Somebody Stole My Guitar 4:08   Purpendicular
- The Purpendicular Waltz 4:43   Purpendicular
- Pictured Within (Live)   8:42   In Concert With The London Symphony Orchestra (Live)
- Wait A While (Live)   6:49   In Concert With The London Symphony Orchestra (Live)
- Sitting In A Dream (Live) 3:53   In Concert With The London Symphony Orchestra (Live)
- Love Is All (Live)   4:39   In Concert With The London Symphony Orchestra (Live)
- Via Miami (Live)   4:56   In Concert With The London Symphony Orchestra (Live)

- That's Why God Is Singing The Blues (Live)   3:58
  In Concert With The London Symphony Orchestra (Live)
- Take It Off The Top (Live)   4:38   In Concert With The
  London Symphony Orchestra (Live)
- Wring That Neck (Live)   4:36   In Concert With The
  London Symphony Orchestra (Live)
- Pictures Of Home (Live)   9:26   In Concert With The
  London Symphony Orchestra (Live)
- Concerto For Group And Orchestra - Movement I (Live)
  17:04   In Concert With The London Symphony
  Orchestra (Live)
- Concerto For Group And Orchestra - Movement II (Live)
  19:43   In Concert With The London Symphony
  Orchestra (Live)
- Concerto For Group And Orchestra - Movement III
  (Live)   13:28   In Concert With The London
  Symphony Orchestra (Live)
- Ted The Mechanic (Live)   4:50   In Concert With The
  London Symphony Orchestra (Live)
- Watching The Sky (Live)   5:38   In Concert With The
  London Symphony Orchestra (Live)
- Sometimes I Feel Like Screaming (Live)   7:44   In
  Concert With The London Symphony Orchestra (Live)
- Smoke On The Water (Live)   6:44   In Concert
  With The London Symphony Orchestra (Live)
- Money Talks   5:34   Rapture of the Deep
- Girls Like That   4:01   Rapture of the Deep
- Wrong Man4:52   Rapture of the Deep

- Rapture of the Deep   5:57   Rapture of the Deep
- Clearly Quite Absurd   5:23   Rapture of the Deep
- Don't Let Go   4:34   Rapture of the Deep
- Back to Back   4:05   Rapture of the Deep
- Kiss Tomorrow Goodbye   4:19   Rapture of the Deep
- Junkyard Blues   5:34   Rapture of the Deep
- Before Time Began 6:32   Rapture of the Deep
- A Simple Song   4:39   Now What?!
- Weirdistan 4:14   Now What?!
- Out of Hand 6:10   Now What?!
- Hell to Pay   5:11   Now What?!
- Body Line   4:26   Now What?!
- Above and Beyond 5:30   Now What?!
- Blood from a Stone 5:18   Now What?!
- Uncommon Man   7:00   Now What?!
- Aprèz vous   5:26   Now What?!
- All the Time in the World   4:21   Now What?!
- Vincent Price   4:46   Now What?!
- Time for Bedlam   4:35   Infinite (Bonus Track Version)
- Hip Boots   3:23   Infinite (Bonus Track Version)
- All I Got Is You   4:42   Infinite (Bonus Track Version)
- One Night In Vegas 3:23   Infinite (Bonus Track Version)
- Get Me Outta Here 3:58   Infinite (Bonus Track Version)
- The Surprising   5:57   Infinite (Bonus Track Version)
- Johnny's Band   3:51   Infinite (Bonus Track Version)
- On Top of the World   4:01   Infinite (Bonus Track Version)
- Birds of Prey   5:47   Infinite (Bonus Track Version)

- Roadhouse Blues   6:00   Infinite (Bonus Track Version)
- Paradise Bar 4:10   Infinite (Bonus Track Version)
- Uncommon Man (Instrumental Version)   6:58   Infinite (Bonus Track Version)
- Hip Boots (Ian Paice Recording)   4:00   Infinite (Bonus Track Version)
- Strange Kind of Woman (Live In Alborg) 5:46   Infinite (Bonus Track Version)
- Throw My Bones   3:38   Whoosh!
- Drop the Weapon   4:23   Whoosh!
- We're All the Same In the Dark   3:44   Whoosh!
- Nothing at All   4:42   Whoosh!
- No Need to Shout   3:30   Whoosh!
- Step By Step 3:34   Whoosh!
- What the What   3:32   Whoosh!
- The Long Way Round   5:39   Whoosh!
- The Power of the Moon   4:08   Whoosh!
- Remission Possible 1:38   Whoosh!
- Man Alive   5:35   Whoosh!
- And the Address (2020 Version)   3:35   Whoosh!
- Dancing In My Sleep   3:51   Whoosh!
- 7 and 7 Is   2:28   Turning to Crime
- Rockin' Pneumonia and the Boogie Woogie Flu   3:15 Turning to Crime
- Oh Well   4:31   Turning to Crime
- Jenny Take a Ride! 4:36   Turning to Crime
- Watching the River Flow   3:02   Turning to Crime
- Let the Good Times Roll   4:22   Turning to Crime

- Dixie Chicken   4:43   Turning to Crime
- Shapes of Things   3:40   Turning to Crime
- The Battle of New Orleans   2:51   Turning to Crime
- Lucifer   3:45   Turning to Crime
- White Room   4:53   Turning to Crime
- Caught in the Act (Going Down / Green Onions / Hot 'Lanta / Dazed and Confused / Gimme Some Lovin') 7:49 Turning to Crime
- Woman from Tokyo (Live) 6:14   Live In Newcastle 2001
- Ted the Mechanic (Live)   5:11   Live In Newcastle 2001
- Mary Long (Live)   5:56   Live In Newcastle 2001
- Lazy (Live) 6:03   Live In Newcastle 2001
- No One Came (Live)   5:38   Live In Newcastle 2001
- Black Night (Live) 7:22   Live In Newcastle 2001
- Sometimes I Feel Like Screaming (Live)   7:27   Live In Newcastle 2001
- Fools (Live) 9:24   Live In Newcastle 2001
- Perfect Strangers (Live)   9:30   Live In Newcastle 2001
- Hey Cisco (Live)   6:20   Live In Newcastle 2001
- When a Blind Man Cries (Live)   7:27   Live In Newcastle 2001
- Smoke On the Water (Live)10:21   Live In Newcastle 2001

- Speed King / Good Times (Live)   16:59   Live In Newcastle 2001
- Hush (Live) 4:17   Live In Newcastle 2001
- Highway Star (Live)7:23   Live In Newcastle 2001
- Time for Bedlam (Live at Hellfest, 2017)   4:59   The Infinite Live Recordings, Vol. 1
- Fireball (Live at Hellfest, 2017)   3:26   The Infinite Live Recordings, Vol. 1
- Bloodsucker (Live at Hellfest, 2017)4:11   The Infinite Live Recordings, Vol. 1
- Strange Kind of Woman (Live at Hellfest, 2017)   7:41 The Infinite Live Recordings, Vol. 1
- Uncommon Man (Live at Hellfest, 2017)   6:40   The Infinite Live Recordings, Vol. 1
- The Surprising (Live at Hellfest, 2017)   6:01   The Infinite Live Recordings, Vol. 1
- Lazy (Live at Hellfest, 2017)7:47   The Infinite Live Recordings, Vol. 1
- Birds of Prey (Live at Hellfest, 2017)   5:45   The Infinite Live Recordings, Vol. 1
- Hell to Pay (Live at Hellfest, 2017) 5:10   The Infinite Live Recordings, Vol. 1
- Key Solo (Live at Hellfest, 2017)   4:18   The Infinite Live Recordings, Vol. 1
- Perfect Strangers (Live at Hellfest, 2017)   6:29   The Infinite Live Recordings, Vol. 1
- Space Truckin' (Live at Hellfest, 2017)   5:02   The Infinite Live Recordings, Vol. 1

- Smoke on the Water (Live at Hellfest, 2017)   6:40
  The Infinite Live Recordings, Vol. 1
- Peter Gunn / Hush (Live at Hellfest, 2017) 7:40   The
  Infinite Live Recordings, Vol. 1
- Black Night (Live at Hellfest, 2017) 7:25   The Infinite
  Live Recordings, Vol. 1

Playlist: Bolin

Deep Purple's lineup in 1975-76 featured Jon Lord, Ian Paice, Ian Gillan, Glenn Hughes, and the talented guitarist Tommy Bolin. During this period, Deep Purple released the album "Come Taste the Band," which showcased their exploration of funk and soul influences. However, it's essential to understand the context behind Tommy Bolin's inclusion in the band and the departure of Ritchie Blackmore.

Ritchie Blackmore, Deep Purple's iconic guitarist, decided to leave the band in 1975 due to creative differences and a desire to pursue his own musical direction. This left a significant void in the group, which was filled by the virtuosic Tommy Bolin. Bolin brought a fresh perspective and diverse musical influences to Deep Purple, adding a new dimension to their sound.

In addition to his tenure with Deep Purple, Tommy Bolin pursued a solo career, leaving behind a collection of remarkable albums that showcase his immense talent and musical versatility. Let's explore some of Tommy Bolin's solo efforts during this period:

"Teaser":
Released in 1975, "Teaser" stands as Tommy Bolin's most renowned solo album. The record encompasses a fusion of rock, jazz, and funk, showcasing Bolin's impressive guitar skills and songwriting abilities. Tracks like "Post Toastee" and "Wild Dogs" highlight his musical prowess and distinct artistic vision.

"Private Eyes":
Released in 1976, "Private Eyes" further demonstrates Bolin's ability to fuse different genres seamlessly. The album features a mix of hard rock, blues, and soul influences, with tracks like "Bustin' Out for Rosey" and "Gypsy Soul" showcasing Bolin's dynamic guitar work and emotive songwriting.

"The Tommy Bolin Band Live 9/19/76":
Capturing the energy of Bolin's live performances, this live album immortalizes a concert from September 19, 1976. The recording showcases Bolin's incredible stage presence and improvisational skills, offering fans a glimpse into his captivating live performances.

"Acoustic Bolin - EP":
Released posthumously in 1996, this EP highlights a different side of Tommy Bolin's musical talent. Stripping down the arrangements to acoustic guitars, Bolin delivers intimate and heartfelt performances, including renditions of songs like "Alexis" and "Lotus."

Tommy Bolin's contributions to Deep Purple and his solo career were tragically cut short. Bolin struggled with substance abuse, which ultimately led to his untimely death in 1976 at the age of 25. His legacy as a gifted guitarist and visionary artist lives on through his recordings and the impact he made during his time with Deep Purple and as a solo artist.

Tommy Bolin's inclusion in Deep Purple brought a unique flavor to the band's sound, infusing it with his diverse influences and showcasing his immense talent. Despite his brief time with the group, Bolin's contributions and his solo efforts left an indelible mark on the rock music landscape, solidifying his status as a remarkable musician whose potential was tragically cut short.

- Comin' Home   3:56   Come Taste the Band
- Lady Luck   2:47   Come Taste the Band
- Gettin' Tighter   3:38   Come Taste the Band
- Dealer   3:50   Come Taste the Band
- I Need Love 4:23   Come Taste the Band
- Drifter   4:02   Come Taste the Band
- Love Child 3:08   Come Taste the Band

- This Time Around / Owed to 'G'   6:10   Come Taste the Band
- You Keep On Moving   5:22   Come Taste the Band
- People, People   8:01   Come Taste the Man (Original Recording Remastered)
- In His Own Words 0:10   Come Taste the Man (Original Recording Remastered)
- Meaning of Love   3:42   Come Taste the Man (Original Recording Remastered)
- Goin' Down 5:29   Come Taste the Man (Original Recording Remastered)
- In His Own Words 2   0:22   Come Taste the Man (Original Recording Remastered)
- Cross the River   7:10   Come Taste the Man (Original Recording Remastered)
- Teaser   4:01   Come Taste the Man (Original Recording Remastered)
- Gotta Dance   2:43   Come Taste the Man (Original Recording Remastered)
- In His Own Words 3   0:44   Come Taste the Man (Original Recording Remastered)
- Jammin'   2:59   Come Taste the Man (Original Recording Remastered)
- Sky Sail   5:16   Come Taste the Man (Original Recording Remastered)
- In His Own Words 4   0:47   Come Taste the Man (Original Recording Remastered)

- Post Toastee13:17   Come Taste the Man (Original Recording Remastered)
- Rock-a-Bye 3:37   Come Taste the Man (Original Recording Remastered)
- Bustin' Out for Rosey   4:20   Private Eyes
- Sweet Burgundy   4:11   Private Eyes
- Post Toastee9:00   Private Eyes
- Shake the Devil   3:44   Private Eyes
- Gypsy Soul 4:02   Private Eyes
- Someday Will Bring Our Love Home   3:02   Private Eyes
- Hello, Again3:36   Private Eyes
- You Told Me That You Loved Me 5:13   Private Eyes
- Teaser (Live)   6:20   Live at Ebbets Field 5/13/76 (Original Recording Remastered)
- People People (Live)   8:00   Live at Ebbets Field 5/13/76 (Original Recording Remastered)
- The Grind (Live)   3:21   Live at Ebbets Field 5/13/76 (Original Recording Remastered)
- Wild Dogs (Live)   9:01   Live at Ebbets Field 5/13/76 (Original Recording Remastered)
- Delightful (Live)   5:03   Live at Ebbets Field 5/13/76 (Original Recording Remastered)
- I Fell in Love (Live) 5:40   Live at Ebbets Field 5/13/76 (Original Recording Remastered)
- Marching Powder (Live)   14:42   Live at Ebbets Field 5/13/76 (Original Recording Remastered)

- Lotus (Live) 7:06   Live at Ebbets Field 5/13/76 (Original Recording Remastered)
- Homeward Strut (Live)   9:01   Live at Ebbets Field 5/13/76 (Original Recording Remastered)
- Show Intro (Live)   0:21   The Tommy Bolin Band Live 9/19/76
- Teaser (Live)   6:03   The Tommy Bolin Band Live 9/19/76
- People, People (Live)   8:16   The Tommy Bolin Band Live 9/19/76
- You Told Me That You Loved Me (Live)   5:10   The Tommy Bolin Band Live 9/19/76
- Band Intro/Tuning (Live)   3:30   The Tommy Bolin Band Live 9/19/76
- Shake the Devil (Live)   5:26   The Tommy Bolin Band Live 9/19/76
- Keyboard Solo (Live)   2:17   The Tommy Bolin Band Live 9/19/76
- Drum Solo (Live)   2:32   The Tommy Bolin Band Live 9/19/76
- Post Toastee (Live) 12:41   The Tommy Bolin Band Live 9/19/76
- Slow Driver (Remix)   3:34   Acoustic Bolin - EP
- Alexis (Remix)   4:25   Acoustic Bolin - EP
- Teaser (Remix)   3:24   Acoustic Bolin - EP
- Spanish Lover (Remix/Edit)   4:22   Acoustic Bolin - EP
- Smooth Fandango 6:13   Teaser

Playlist: Others Purples

As individual members of Deep Purple pursued their own musical endeavors, they showcased their unique talents and artistic visions through a diverse range of albums. Let's explore some of the notable releases from the band members' solo careers:

"Stranger In Us All" (1995) - Ritchie Blackmore's Rainbow: Ritchie Blackmore's post-Deep Purple band, Rainbow, released "Stranger In Us All," an album that showcased Blackmore's signature guitar work and melodic songwriting. Tracks like "Black Masquerade" and "Ariel" highlighted Blackmore's ability to craft captivating hard rock anthems.

"Danger - White Men Dancing" (feat. Jon Lord): Jon Lord, the legendary Deep Purple keyboardist, collaborated on the album "Danger - White Men Dancing," showcasing his versatility as a musician. The record blended rock, jazz, and classical elements, with Lord's intricate keyboard melodies and improvisations taking center stage.

"Jesus Christ Superstar" (Original Studio Cast):
Ian Gillan, Deep Purple's iconic vocalist, played a pivotal role in the original studio cast recording of the legendary rock opera "Jesus Christ Superstar." His powerful vocal performances on tracks like "Gethsemane (I Only Want to Say)" added depth and emotion to the production.

"Raving with Ian Gillan & The Javelins":
Ian Gillan's album "Raving with Ian Gillan & The Javelins" showcased his love for early rock 'n' roll. The record featured energetic renditions of classic rock 'n' roll tracks, paying homage to Gillan's musical roots and his passion for the genre.

One notable solo effort from Ian Gillan, the iconic vocalist of Deep Purple, is the live album **"Smoke On the Water - Live."** Released as part of his solo career, this album captures Gillan's electrifying stage presence and powerful vocals. With the immortalized track "Smoke On the Water" as a centerpiece, the album showcases Gillan's ability to deliver an unforgettable live performance, filled with energy and passion. This release serves as a testament to Gillan's enduring musical legacy and his mastery of captivating audiences with his dynamic voice.

"E-thnik" - Glenn Hughes:
Glenn Hughes, Deep Purple's former bassist and vocalist, released "E-thnik," an album that explored his diverse musical influences. Blending elements of funk, rock, and

soul, Hughes showcased his powerful vocals and songwriting prowess.

"Live In London 1977" - David Coverdale:
David Coverdale, Deep Purple's former vocalist, released "Live In London 1977," capturing a dynamic live performance. With tracks like "Mistreated" and "Fool for Your Loving," Coverdale demonstrated his commanding stage presence and soulful delivery.

"The Butterfly Ball and the Grasshopper's Feast" - Roger Glover:
Roger Glover, Deep Purple's talented bassist, composed and produced "The Butterfly Ball and the Grasshopper's Feast." This concept album featured a diverse range of artists and showcased Glover's songwriting skills, weaving together an enchanting musical journey.

"Northwinds" (Bonus Track Version) - David Coverdale:
As a solo artist, David Coverdale released "Northwinds," an album that highlighted his soulful vocals and bluesy songwriting. The bonus track version includes additional tracks that further exemplify Coverdale's musical artistry.

"Burning Japan Live" - Tommy Bolin:
"Burning Japan Live" captured the electrifying energy of Tommy Bolin's live performances. The album showcased Bolin's virtuoso guitar skills and diverse musical influences, leaving a lasting testament to his talents

- Wolf to the Moon 4:16   Ritchie Blackmore's Rainbow
  Stranger In Us All
- Cold Hearted Woman   4:30   Ritchie Blackmore's
  Rainbow   Stranger In Us All
- Hunting Humans (Insatiable)   5:44   Ritchie
  Blackmore's Rainbow   Stranger In Us All
- Stand and Fight   5:21   Ritchie Blackmore's Rainbow
  Stranger In Us All
- Ariel   5:39   Ritchie Blackmore's Rainbow
  Stranger In Us All
- Too Late for Tears 4:54   Ritchie Blackmore's Rainbow
  Stranger In Us All
- Black Masquerade   5:35   Ritchie Blackmore's Rainbow
  Stranger In Us All
- Silence   4:04   Ritchie Blackmore's Rainbow
  Stranger In Us All
- Hall of the Mountain King 5:31   Ritchie Blackmore's
  Rainbow   Stranger In Us All
- Still I'm Sad 5:24   Ritchie Blackmore's Rainbow
  Stranger In Us All
- The Blues Just Got Sadder 3:33   The Hoochie Coochie
  Men Danger - White Men Dancing (feat. Jon Lord)
- Gotta Find Me Some Fire 3:57   The Hoochie Coochie
  Men Danger - White Men Dancing (feat. Jon Lord)
- Twisted System   4:14   The Hoochie Coochie Men
  Danger - White Men Dancing (feat. Jon Lord)
- Over & Over   8:07   The Hoochie Coochie Men
  Danger - White Men Dancing (feat. Jon Lord)

- Let It Go   4:16   The Hoochie Coochie Men   Danger - White Men Dancing (feat. Jon Lord)
- Heart of Stone   3:50   The Hoochie Coochie Men Danger - White Men Dancing (feat. Jon Lord)
- If This Ain't the Blues   6:29   The Hoochie Coochie Men Danger - White Men Dancing (feat. Jon Lord)
- Danger White Men Dancing   4:33   The Hoochie Coochie Men   Danger - White Men Dancing (feat. Jon Lord)
- Dead Presidents   2:45   The Hoochie Coochie Men Danger - White Men Dancing (feat. Jon Lord)
- Hoochie Coochie Man   4:35   The Hoochie Coochie Men Danger - White Men Dancing (feat. Jon Lord)
- Bottle O' Wine   4:58   The Hoochie Coochie Men Danger - White Men Dancing (feat. Jon Lord)
- Everybody Wants to Go to Heaven 4:24   The Hoochie Coochie Men   Danger - White Men Dancing (feat. Jon Lord)
- Tell Your Story Walkin'   4:41   The Hoochie Coochie Men Danger - White Men Dancing (feat. Jon Lord)
- If This Ain't the Blues (Bonus Track)   6:37   The Hoochie Coochie Men   Danger - White Men Dancing (feat. Jon Lord)
- Hoochie Coochie Man (Bonus Track)   4:36   The Hoochie Coochie Men   Danger - White Men Dancing (feat. Jon Lord)
- Smoke On the Water (Re-Recorded)   8:06   The Ian Gillian Band   1970's: Rockin' Flashback, Vol. 4

- O nainana' 5:03 Ian Paice & Mario Fasciano E-thnik
- Simon Zealotes / Poor Jerusalem 4:47 John Gustafson & Ian Gillan Jesus Christ Superstar (Original Studio Cast)
- Too Much Monkey Business 2:58 Ian Gillan Raving with Ian Gillan & The Javelins
- It'll Be Me 1:58 Ian Gillan Raving with Ian Gillan & The Javelins
- You Really Got a Hold on Me 2:58 Ian Gillan Raving with Ian Gillan & The Javelins
- Its Only Make Believe 2:14 Ian Gillan Raving with Ian Gillan & The Javelins
- Can I Get a Witness 3:02 Ian Gillan Raving with Ian Gillan & The Javelins
- Poison Ivy 2:09 Ian Gillan Raving with Ian Gillan & The Javelins
- Rave On 1:53 Ian Gillan Raving with Ian Gillan & The Javelins
- Blue Monday 2:25 Ian Gillan Raving with Ian Gillan & The Javelins
- You Better Move On 2:42 Ian Gillan Raving with Ian Gillan & The Javelins
- Somethin Else 2:06 Ian Gillan Raving with Ian Gillan & The Javelins
- Money 2:50 Ian Gillan Raving with Ian Gillan & The Javelins

- Love Potion No. 9 2:08 Ian Gillan Raving with Ian Gillan & The Javelins
- Lets Dance 2:29 Ian Gillan Raving with Ian Gillan & The Javelins
- Roll over Beethoven 2:46 Ian Gillan Raving with Ian Gillan & The Javelins
- Clear Air Turbulence (Live) 5:25 Ian Gillan Smoke On the Water - Live
- Money Lender (Live) 4:45 Ian Gillan Smoke On the Water - Live
- Child In Time (Live) 8:51 Ian Gillan Smoke On the Water - Live
- Smoke On the Water (Live) 8:06 Ian Gillan Smoke On the Water - Live
- Woman from Tokyo (Live) 4:07 Ian Gillan Smoke On the Water - Live
- Twin Exhausted (Live) 5:28 Ian Gillan Smoke On the Water - Live
- La notte delle stelle 1:57 Ian Paice & Mario Fasciano E-thnik
- Tarantella a dispetto 3:04 Ian Paice & Mario Fasciano E-thnik
- L'amore quando c'e' 5:06 Ian Paice & Mario Fasciano E-thnik
- Che sogno 3:27 Ian Paice & Mario Fasciano E-thnik
- A notte 4:19 Ian Paice & Mario Fasciano E-thnik

- Sulo 3:28   Ian Paice & Mario Fasciano   E-thnik
- Tu si' accussi'   3:02   Ian Paice & Mario Fasciano   E-thnik
- L'ala della musica   4:44   Ian Paice & Mario Fasciano   E-thnik
- O mare e l'anema   4:27   Ian Paice & Mario Fasciano   E-thnik
- A Ghost Story (Live)   4:34   Paice, Ashton, Lord   Live In London 1977
- On the Road Again. Again (Live)   5:26   Paice, Ashton, Lord   Live In London 1977
- Silas & Jerome (Live)   4:01   Paice, Ashton, Lord   Live In London 1977
- Arrabella (Live)   4:44   Paice, Ashton, Lord   Live In London 1977
- The Ballad of Mr. Giver (Live)   7:29   Paice, Ashton, Lord   Live In London 1977
- I'm Gonna Stop Drinkin' (Live)   5:17   Paice, Ashton, Lord   Live In London 1977
- Steamroller (Live)   5:22   Paice, Ashton, Lord   Live In London 1977
- Remember the Good Times (Live) 6:30   Paice, Ashton, Lord   Live In London 1977
- Sneaky Private Lee (Live)   7:39   Paice, Ashton, Lord   Live In London 1977
- Dawn   1:20   Roger Glover   The Butterfly Ball and the Grasshopper's Feast

- Get Ready   2:07   Roger Glover & Glenn Hughes
  The Butterfly Ball and the Grasshopper's Feast
- Saffron Dormouse & Lizzy Bee   1:22   Roger Glover,
  Helen Chapelle & Barry St. John   The Butterfly Ball and
  the Grasshopper's Feast
- Harlequin Hare   1:27   Roger Glover & Neil
  Lancaster   The Butterfly Ball and the Grasshopper's
  Feast
- Old Blind Mole   1:12   Roger Glover & John
  Goodison   The Butterfly Ball and the Grasshopper's
  Feast
- Magician Moth   1:34   Roger Glover   The Butterfly
  Ball and the Grasshopper's Feast
- No Solution 3:28   Roger Glover & Micky Lee Soule
  The Butterfly Ball and the Grasshopper's Feast
- Behind the Smile   1:46   Roger Glover & David
  Coverdale   The Butterfly Ball and the Grasshopper's
  Feast
- Fly Away   2:22   Roger Glover & Liza Strike   The
  Butterfly Ball and the Grasshopper's Feast
- Aranea   1:37   Roger Glover & Judi Kuhl   The
  Butterfly Ball and the Grasshopper's Feast
- Sitting In a Dream 3:40   Roger Glover & Ronnie James
  Dio The Butterfly Ball and the Grasshopper's Feast
- Waiting   3:11   Roger Glover & Jimmy Helms The
  Butterfly Ball and the Grasshopper's Feast
- Sir Maximus Mouse 2:34   Roger Glover & Eddie Hardin
  The Butterfly Ball and the Grasshopper's Feast

- Dreams of Sir Bedivere   4:09   Roger Glover   The Butterfly Ball and the Grasshopper's Feast
- Together Again   2:05   Roger Glover & Tony Ashton The Butterfly Ball and the Grasshopper's Feast
- Watch Out for the Bat   1:41   Roger Glover & John Gustafson   The Butterfly Ball and the Grasshopper's Feast
- Little Chalk Blue   3:45   Roger Glover & John Lawton The Butterfly Ball and the Grasshopper's Feast
- The Feast   1:48   Roger Glover   The Butterfly Ball and the Grasshopper's Feast
- Love Is All   3:14   Roger Glover & Ronnie James Dio The Butterfly Ball and the Grasshopper's Feast
- Homeward   4:13   Roger Glover & Ronnie James Dio The Butterfly Ball and the Grasshopper's Feast
- Love Is All (Demo Version) 3:07   Roger Glover   The Butterfly Ball and the Grasshopper's Feast
- Dawn (Alternate Mix)   1:36   Roger Glover   The Butterfly Ball and the Grasshopper's Feast
- Magician Moth (Alternate Mix)   1:39   Roger Glover The Butterfly Ball and the Grasshopper's Feast
- Harlequin Hare (Alternate Mix)   1:35   Roger Glover The Butterfly Ball and the Grasshopper's Feast
- Magician Moth (Alternate Mix 2)   1:34   Roger Glover The Butterfly Ball and the Grasshopper's Feast
- No Solution (Alternate Mix)   4:00   Roger Glover The Butterfly Ball and the Grasshopper's Feast

- Waiting (Alternate Mix)   3:12   Roger Glover   The Butterfly Ball and the Grasshopper's Feast
- Fly Away (Alternate Mix)   2:24   Roger Glover   The Butterfly Ball and the Grasshopper's Feast
- Aranea (Alternate Mix)   1:37   Roger Glover   The Butterfly Ball and the Grasshopper's Feast
- Paranormal (feat. Roger Glover)   4:11   Alice Cooper Paranormal
- Lonely Avenue   3:09   Ian Gillan & Roger Glover Rain Man (Original Motion Picture Soundtrack)
- Keep On Giving Me Love   5:16   David Coverdale Northwinds (Bonus Track Version)
- Northwinds 6:13   David Coverdale   Northwinds (Bonus Track Version)
- Give Me Kindness   4:34   David Coverdale Northwinds (Bonus Track Version)
- Time & Again   4:02   David Coverdale Northwinds (Bonus Track Version)
- Queen of Hearts   5:16   David Coverdale Northwinds (Bonus Track Version)
- Only My Soul   4:36   David Coverdale Northwinds (Bonus Track Version)
- Say You Love Me   4:21   David Coverdale Northwinds (Bonus Track Version)
- Breakdown 5:15   David Coverdale   Northwinds (Bonus Track Version)
- Shame the Devil (Bonus Track)   3:35   David Coverdale   Northwinds (Bonus Track Version)

- Sweet Mistreater (Bonus Track)   3:45   David
  Coverdale   Northwinds (Bonus Track Version)
- Burn (Live) 6:44   Glenn Hughes Burning Japan Live
- The Liar (Live)   4:39   Glenn Hughes Burning Japan
  Live
- Muscle and Blood (Live)   5:48   Glenn Hughes
  Burning Japan Live
- Lay My Body Down (Live) 5:08   Glenn Hughes
  Burning Japan Live
- From Now On... (Live)   6:08   Glenn Hughes
  Burning Japan Live
- Into the Void (Live) 7:13   Glenn Hughes Burning Japan
  Live
- Still in Love with You (Live)   2:10   Glenn Hughes
  Burning Japan Live
- Coast to Coast (Live)   6:52   Glenn Hughes
  Burning Japan Live
- This Time Around (Live)   3:32   Glenn Hughes
  Burning Japan Live
- Owed to H (Live)   2:53   Glenn Hughes Burning Japan
  Live
- Gettin' Tighter (Live)   3:59   Glenn Hughes
  Burning Japan Live
- You Keep on Moving (Live)   7:25   Glenn Hughes
  Burning Japan Live
- Lady Double Dealer (Live) 3:45   Glenn Hughes
  Burning Japan Live

- I Got Your Number (Live) 4:17   Glenn Hughes
  Burning Japan Live
- Stormbringer (Live)   5:10   Glenn Hughes
  Burning Japan Live
- Teaser (Live)   5:51   Tommy Bolin   Tommy Bolin
  Lives!
- Red Skies   8:09   Tommy Bolin   Tommy Bolin Lives!
- Alexis (Acoustic Demo)   4:26   Tommy Bolin
  Tommy Bolin Lives!
- Cucumber Jam   8:10   Tommy Bolin   Tommy Bolin
  Lives!
- Stratus (Live Ebbets Field 11/74)   11:10   Tommy Bolin
  Tommy Bolin Lives!
- Wild Dogs (Acoustic Demo)   4:44   Tommy Bolin
  Tommy Bolin Lives!
- People, People (Live Remastered from Ebbbets Field)
  8:10 Tommy Bolin   Tommy Bolin Lives!
- Lotus (Live) 6:25   Tommy Bolin   Tommy Bolin Lives!
- Savannah Woman   3:43   Tommy Bolin   Tommy Bolin
  Lives!
- Post Toastee (Live) 10:35   Tommy Bolin   Tommy Bolin
  Lives!

Status Quo

Status Quo is a British rock band that has achieved remarkable success and longevity since its formation in 1962. Originally known as "The Spectres," the group underwent several lineup changes before eventually settling on its classic formation, consisting of Francis Rossi, Rick Parfitt, Alan Lancaster, John Coghlan, and Andy Bown.

The band's early sound was heavily influenced by the British beat and psychedelic rock movements of the 1960s. However, it was in the early 1970s that Status Quo found their signature style and became renowned for their distinctive boogie rock sound. Characterized by powerful guitar riffs, driving rhythm sections, and catchy melodies, their music often featured a 12-bar blues structure.

Status Quo's breakthrough came with the release of their hit single "Pictures of Matchstick Men" in 1968, which reached the top ten in the UK charts and helped establish their reputation as a prominent rock band. Throughout the 1970s, they achieved a string of successful albums and singles, including "Caroline," "Down Down," and "Rockin' All Over the World," which solidified their status as one of Britain's most beloved rock acts.

The 1980s and 1990s brought some lineup changes, with various members departing and new musicians joining the fold. However, Rossi and Parfitt remained the core of the group, continuing to tour extensively and release new material. The band's live performances were known for their high energy and infectious enthusiasm, often featuring their iconic "double-neck" guitars and relentless stage presence.

Tragically, Rick Parfitt passed away in December 2016, marking a significant loss for both the band and their fans. Despite the profound impact of his absence, the band decided to carry on in Parfitt's memory, with guitarist Richie Malone joining as his replacement. The surviving members continued to tour and released a critically acclaimed album titled "Backbone" in 2019.

Status Quo's enduring popularity can be attributed to their steadfast dedication to its unique brand of rock music. Over the course of their career, they have released numerous studio albums, live recordings, and compilations, collectively selling millions of records worldwide. Their influence on rock music and their ability to connect with audiences has earned them a devoted fan base and a rightful place in the annals of British rock history.

Despite the passing of some original members, Status Quo remains an active band, determined to keep the spirit and legacy of their music alive. With their timeless hits and captivating live performances, they continue to entertain and inspire generations of rock fans around the globe.

Playlist: Status Quo 1

"Picturesque Matchstickable Messages from the Status Quo"
In the psychedelic haze of the late '60s, a band emerged with a sound that was both rebellious and infectious. Status Quo's debut album, "Picturesque Matchstickable Messages from the Status Quo," captured the essence of the era, blending groovy

melodies, swirling harmonies, and a healthy dose of British rock 'n' roll swagger. From the moment the needle hits the vinyl, the album takes you on a kaleidoscopic journey through a world of swirling colors and whimsical lyrics, inviting you to embrace the musical revolution of the time.

"The Technicolor Dreams of the Status Quo"
If there ever was an album that could transport you to a vibrant dreamscape of sound, it's "The Technicolor Dreams of the Status Quo." Bursting with kaleidoscopic melodies and infectious rhythms, this album is a sonic tapestry that weaves together the best of psychedelic rock, pop, and blues. From the mind-bending guitar solos to the infectious harmonies, Status Quo paints a vivid musical landscape that immerses you in a technicolor whirlwind of sonic delights. Surrender yourself to the dreamscape and let the music guide you through a world of boundless imagination.

"The Complete Pye Collection"
Step into the time machine and journey back to the heyday of British rock 'n' roll with "The Complete Pye Collection" by Status Quo. This comprehensive anthology is a treasure trove of the band's early hits, capturing their raw energy and their ability to infuse infectious melodies into every note. From the foot-stomping rhythms of "Down the Dustpipe" to the gritty blues-rock of "Mean Girl," this collection is a testament to Status Quo's musical prowess and their undeniable place in rock history. Immerse yourself in the sounds of an era that defined a generation.

"Spare Parts"
The engine of rock 'n' roll is fueled by innovation, and Status Quo's "Spare Parts" is a testament to their creative drive.

This expanded edition of their classic album showcases the band's evolution, as they push the boundaries of their signature sound while staying true to their rock roots. With a mix of hard-hitting anthems and introspective ballads, "Spare Parts" delves into the depths of the human experience, tackling themes of love, loss, and the relentless pursuit of dreams. Prepare to be captivated by the raw emotion and musical craftsmanship that makes this album a true gem in Status Quo's discography.

"Down the Dustpipe"
From the gritty backstreets of rock 'n' roll, where the amplifiers roar and the guitars howl, comes "Down the Dustpipe" by Status Quo. This album is a no-frills, foot-stomping collection of blues-infused rock that hits you like a freight train. With its infectious riffs, driving rhythms, and Francis Rossi's unmistakable gravelly vocals, "Down the Dustpipe" is a high-octane ride through the heart and soul of rock music. Buckle up, turn up the volume, and get ready to groove to the timeless sound of Status Quo.

"Ma Kelly's Greasy Spoon"
When the hunger for gritty rock 'n' roll strikes, "Ma Kelly's Greasy Spoon" is the place to satisfy your cravings. Status Quo serves up a heaping plate of blues-infused boogie that's dripping with raw energy and a rebellious spirit. From the infectious grooves of "Spinning Wheel Blues" to the soulful swagger of "Lazy Poker Blues," this album is a greasy, no-frills feast that will leave you hungry for more. Grab a seat at Ma Kelly's, order up a dose of pure rock 'n' roll, and let the music wash over you like sonic comfort food. It's time to indulge in the flavors of Status Quo.

"Hello"

When Status Quo says "Hello," the world listens. This iconic album is a triumph of British rock 'n' roll, featuring the band at the peak of their powers. From the undeniable swagger of the title track to the infectious hooks of "Roll Over Lay Down," Status Quo delivers an adrenaline-fueled, foot-stomping experience that will have you on your feet from start to finish. "Hello" is a timeless testament to the band's ability to create anthems that ignite stadiums and unite generations. So get ready to raise your fist, shout at the top of your lungs, and join the rock 'n' roll revolution. Status Quo has arrived, and they're here to say "Hello."

- Black Veils of Melancholy (Mono Version) 3:16
  Picturesque Matchstickable Messages from the Status Quo
- When My Mind Is Not Live (Mono Version)   2:49
  Picturesque Matchstickable Messages from the Status Quo
- Ice In the Sun (Mono Version)   2:13   Picturesque
  Matchstickable Messages from the Status Quo
- Elizabeth Dreams (Mono Version) 3:28   Picturesque
  Matchstickable Messages from the Status Quo
- Gentleman Joe's Sidewalk Cafe (Mono Version)   3:01
  Picturesque Matchstickable Messages from the Status Quo
- Paradise Flat (Mono Version)   3:13   Picturesque
  Matchstickable Messages from the Status Quo
- Technicolor Dreams (Mono Version)   2:53
  Picturesque Matchstickable Messages from the Status Quo
- Sheila (Mono Version)   1:55   Picturesque
  Matchstickable Messages from the Status Quo

- Spicks and Specks (Mono Version) 2:45   Picturesque Matchstickable Messages from the Status Quo
- Sunny Cellophane Skies (Mono Version)   2:46 Picturesque Matchstickable Messages from the Status Quo
- Green Tambourine (Mono Version)   2:18 Picturesque Matchstickable Messages from the Status Quo
- Pictures of Matchstick Men (Mono Version)   3:10 Picturesque Matchstickable Messages from the Status Quo
- To Be Free (B-Side Version)   2:36   Picturesque Matchstickable Messages from the Status Quo
- Make Me Stay a Little Bit Longer (A-Side Version) 2:55 Picturesque Matchstickable Messages from the Status Quo
- Auntie Nellie (B-Side Version)   3:21   Picturesque Matchstickable Messages from the Status Quo
- Interview With Brian Matthew (BBC Sessions Saturday Club 7/2/1968)   1:07   Picturesque Matchstickable Messages from the Status Quo
- Pictures of Matchstick Men (Live at the BBC)   3:13 Picturesque Matchstickable Messages from the Status Quo
- Things Get Better (BBC Saturday Club 17/2/1968) 2:10 Picturesque Matchstickable Messages from the Status Quo
- Spicks and Specks (Live at the BBC)   2:47 Picturesque Matchstickable Messages from the Status Quo
- Judy In Disguise (BBC Saturday Club 17/2/1968)   2:44 Picturesque Matchstickable Messages from the Status Quo
- Interview With Status Quo (BBC Sessions Saturday Club 17/2/1968) 1:18   Picturesque Matchstickable Messages from the Status Quo

- Make Me Stay a Little Bit Longer (Live at the BBC) 2:48 Picturesque Matchstickable Messages from the Status Quo
- Black Veils of Melancholy (Stereo Remixed 'Proper') 3:15 Picturesque Matchstickable Messages from the Status Quo
- When My Mind Is Not Live (Stereo Version) 3:01 Picturesque Matchstickable Messages from the Status Quo
- Ice in the Sun (Mono Version) 2:12 Picturesque Matchstickable Messages from the Status Quo
- Elizabeth Dreams (Stereo Version) 3:48 Picturesque Matchstickable Messages from the Status Quo
- Gentleman Joe's Sidewalk Cafe (Stereo Version) 3:00 Picturesque Matchstickable Messages from the Status Quo
- Paradise Flat (Stereo Version) 3:14 Picturesque Matchstickable Messages from the Status Quo
- Technicolor Dreams (Stereo Version) 3:18 Picturesque Matchstickable Messages from the Status Quo
- Sheila (Stereo Version) 1:56 Picturesque Matchstickable Messages from the Status Quo
- Spicks and Specks (Stereo Version) 2:54 Picturesque Matchstickable Messages from the Status Quo
- Sunny Cellophane Skies (Stereo Version) 2:48 Picturesque Matchstickable Messages from the Status Quo
- Green Tambourine (Stereo Version) 2:19 Picturesque Matchstickable Messages from the Status Quo
- Pictures of Matchstick Men (Stereo Version) 3:15 Picturesque Matchstickable Messages from the Status Quo

- Auntie Nellie (Stereo Version)   3:31   Picturesque Matchstickable Messages from the Status Quo
- Gloria (BBC Sessions Saturday Club 10/9/1966)   2:46 Picturesque Matchstickable Messages from the Status Quo
- Interview With Francis Rossi (BBC Live Recording) 0:49 Picturesque Matchstickable Messages from the Status Quo
- I (Who Have Nothing) [BBC Live Recording]   3:02 Picturesque Matchstickable Messages from the Status Quo
- Neighbour Neighbour (BBC Live Recording)   2:38 Picturesque Matchstickable Messages from the Status Quo
- I Don't Want You (BBC Session)   2:33   Picturesque Matchstickable Messages from the Status Quo
- Almost But Not Quite There (BBC Session)   2:38 Picturesque Matchstickable Messages from the Status Quo
- Spicks and Specks (Saturday Club BBC Session 24/6/67) 2:46 Picturesque Matchstickable Messages from the Status Quo
- Gloria (BBC David Symonds Show)   2:43 Picturesque Matchstickable Messages from the Status Quo
- Interview With Alan Lancaster (BBC the David Symonds Show April 1968)   1:00   Picturesque Matchstickable Messages from the Status Quo
- Black Veils of Melancholy (BBC David Symonds Show April 1968) 3:14   Picturesque Matchstickable Messages from the Status Quo

- Bloodhound (BBC David Symonds Show April 1968) 2:05 Picturesque Matchstickable Messages from the Status Quo
- I (Who Have Nothing) [Mono Version]   3:03   The Technicolor Dreams of the Status Quo
- Neighbour Neighbour (Mono Version)   2:44   The Technicolor Dreams of the Status Quo
- Hurdy Gurdy Man (Mono Version) 3:17   The Technicolor Dreams of the Status Quo
- Laticia (Mono Version)   3:01   The Technicolor Dreams of the Status Quo
- (We Ain't Got) Nothing Yet [Mono Version]   2:20 The Technicolor Dreams of the Status Quo
- I Want It (Mono Version)   3:03   The Technicolor Dreams of the Status Quo
- Walking With My Angel (Mono Version) 2:16   The Technicolor Dreams of the Status Quo
- When He Passed By (Mono Version)   2:50   The Technicolor Dreams of the Status Quo
- Almost But Not Quite There (Mono Version)   2:46 The Technicolor Dreams of the Status Quo
- Wait a Minute (Mono Version)   2:15   The Technicolor Dreams of the Status Quo
- Pictures of Matchstick Men (Mono Version)   3:14 The Technicolor Dreams of the Status Quo
- Gentleman Joe's Sidewalk Cafe (Mono Version)   3:01 The Technicolor Dreams of the Status Quo

- Black Veils of Melancholy (Mono Version) 3:13   The Technicolor Dreams of the Status Quo
- To Be Free (Mono Version) 2:35   The Technicolor Dreams of the Status Quo
- Ice in the Sun (Mono Version)   2:12   The Technicolor Dreams of the Status Quo
- When My Mind Is Not Live (Mono Version)   2:49 The Technicolor Dreams of the Status Quo
- Elizabeth Dreams (Mono Version) 3:28   The Technicolor Dreams of the Status Quo
- Paradise Flat (Mono Version)   3:12   The Technicolor Dreams of the Status Quo
- Technicolor Dreams (Mono Version)   2:53   The Technicolor Dreams of the Status Quo
- Spicks and Specks (Mono Version) 2:45   The Technicolor Dreams of the Status Quo
- Sheila (Mono Version)   1:55   The Technicolor Dreams of the Status Quo
- Sunny Cellophane Skies (Mono Version)   2:46   The Technicolor Dreams of the Status Quo
- Green Tambourine (Mono Version)   2:17   The Technicolor Dreams of the Status Quo
  Make Me Stay a Little Bit Longer (Mono Version) 2:54 The Technicolor Dreams of the Status Quo
- Auntie Nellie (Mono Version)   3:21   The Technicolor Dreams of the Status Quo
- Are You Growing Tired of My Love (Mono Version) 3:36 The Technicolor Dreams of the Status Quo

- So Ends Another Life (Mono Version)   3:42   The
  Technicolor Dreams of the Status Quo
- Face Without a Soul (Mono Version)   3:08   The
  Technicolor Dreams of the Status Quo
- You're Just What I Was Looking for Today 3:49   The
  Technicolor Dreams of the Status Quo
- Are You Growing Tired of My Love   3:37   The
  Technicolor Dreams of the Status Quo
- Antique Angelique (Mono Version)   3:23   The
  Technicolor Dreams of the Status Quo
- So Ends Another Life   3:11   The Technicolor
  Dreams of the Status Quo
- Poor Old Man (Mono Version)   3:38   The
  Technicolor Dreams of the Status Quo
- Mr. Mind Detector (Mono Version)   4:01   The
  Technicolor Dreams of the Status Quo
- The Clown (Mono Version)   3:24   The
  Technicolor Dreams of the Status Quo
- Velvet Curtains (Mono Version)   2:59   The
  Technicolor Dreams of the Status Quo
- Little Miss Nothing (Stereo Version)   3:02   The
  Technicolor Dreams of the Status Quo
- When I Awake (Mono)   3:51   The Technicolor
  Dreams of the Status Quo
- Nothing At All (Mono Version)   3:54   The
  Technicolor Dreams of the Status Quo
- The Price of Love   3:40   The Technicolor Dreams of
  the Status Quo

- Josie (Mono Version)   3:35   The Technicolor Dreams of the Status Quo
- Do You Live in Fire (Mono Version)   2:13   The Technicolor Dreams of the Status Quo
- Spicks and Specks   2:38   The Technicolor Dreams of the Status Quo
- Pictures of Matchstick Men 3:15   The Technicolor Dreams of the Status Quo
- Paradise Flat   3:14   The Technicolor Dreams of the Status Quo
- Sunny Cellophane Skies   2:47   The Technicolor Dreams of the Status Quo
- Technicolor Dreams   3:16   The Technicolor Dreams of the Status Quo
- Gentleman Joe's Sidewalk Cafe   2:59   The Technicolor Dreams of the Status Quo
- Elizabeth Dreams   3:47   The Technicolor Dreams of the Status Quo
- When My Mind Is Not Live (Stereo Version)   3:00   The Technicolor Dreams of the Status Quo
- Little Miss Nothing (Mono Version)   2:55   The Technicolor Dreams of the Status Quo
- Pictures of Matchstick Men 3:16   The Complete Pye Collection
- Gentleman Joe's Sidewalk Cafe (Mono Version)   3:00   The Complete Pye Collection
- Black Veils of Melancholy 3:13   The Complete Pye Collection

- To Be Free 2:36   The Complete Pye Collection
- Ice in the Sun   2:11   The Complete Pye Collection
- When My Mind Is Not Live (Stereo Version)   3:00
  The Complete Pye Collection
- Elizabeth Dreams 3:47   The Complete Pye Collection
- Paradise Flat (Mono Version)   3:13   The Complete
  Pye Collection
- Technicolor Dreams   3:16   The Complete Pye
  Collection
- Spicks and Specks (Mono Version) 2:52   The Complete
  Pye Collection
- Sheila (Mono Version)   1:54   The Complete Pye
  Collection
- Sunny Cellophane Skies (Mono Version)   2:46   The
  Complete Pye Collection
- Green Tambourine (Mono Version)   2:18   The
  Complete Pye Collection
- Make Me Stay a Little Bit Longer (A-Side Version) 2:53
  The Complete Pye Collection
- Auntie Nellie (B-Side Version)   3:30   The Complete
  Pye Collection
- I (Who Have Nothing) [Mono Version]   3:01   The
  Complete Pye Collection
- Neighbour Neighbour (Mono Version)   2:43   The
  Complete Pye Collection
- Hurdy Gurdy Man (Mono Version) 3:15   The Complete
  Pye Collection
- Laticia   3:01   The Complete Pye Collection

- (We Ain't Got) Nothing Yet [Mono Version]   2:18
  The Complete Pye Collection
- I Want It (Mono Version)   3:02   The Complete Pye
  Collection
- Spicks and Specks   2:38   The Complete Pye Collection
- Almost But Not Quite There   2:45   The Complete
  Pye Collection
- Wait a Minute (Mono Version)   2:14   The Complete
  Pye Collection
- Walking With My Angel   2:14   The Complete Pye
  Collection
- When He Passed By2:50   The Complete Pye Collection
- Are You Growing Tired of My Love (Mono Version)
  3:37 The Complete Pye Collection
- So Ends Another Life   3:11   The Complete Pye
  Collection
- Face Without a Soul   3:07   The Complete Pye
  Collection
- You're Just What I Was Looking for Today 3:48   The
  Complete Pye Collection
- Antique Angelique 3:23   The Complete Pye Collection
- Poor Old Man   3:37   The Complete Pye Collection
- Mr. Mind Detector 4:00   The Complete Pye Collection
- The Clown 3:24   The Complete Pye Collection
- Velvet Curtains   2:59   The Complete Pye Collection
- Little Miss Nothing 3:01   The Complete Pye Collection
- When I Awake   3:51   The Complete Pye Collection
- Nothing At All   3:53   The Complete Pye Collection

- Josie (Out-Take Version)   3:35   The Complete Pye Collection
- Do You Live In Fire 2:13   The Complete Pye Collection
- The Price of Love   3:40   The Complete Pye Collection
- Down the Dustpipe 2:03   The Complete Pye Collection
- Spinning Wheel Blues   3:18   The Complete Pye Collection
- Daughter   3:00   The Complete Pye Collection
- Everything   2:35   The Complete Pye Collection
- Shy Fly   3:46   The Complete Pye Collection
- (April) Spring, Summer & Wednesdays   4:10   The Complete Pye Collection
- Gerdundula 3:21   The Complete Pye Collection
- Junior's Wailing   3:32   The Complete Pye Collection
- Lakky Lady 3:12   The Complete Pye Collection
- Need Your Love   4:44   The Complete Pye Collection
- Lazy Poker Blues   3:35   The Complete Pye Collection
- Is It Really Me / Gotta Go Home   9:30   The Complete Pye Collection
- In My Chair 3:14   The Complete Pye Collection
- Tune to the Music (7" Single Version)   3:06   The Complete Pye Collection
- Good Thinking   3:40   The Complete Pye Collection
- Umleitung 7:10   The Complete Pye Collection
- Something's Going On In My Head 4:44   The Complete Pye Collection
- Mean Girl   3:53   The Complete Pye Collection

- Gerdundula (Alternate Version)   3:48   The Complete
  Pye Collection
- Railroad   5:30   The Complete Pye Collection
- Someone's Learning   7:08   The Complete Pye
  Collection
- Nanana   2:25   The Complete Pye Collection
- Face Without a Soul   3:07   Spare Parts
- You're Just What I Was Looking for Today 3:48   Spare
  Parts
- Are You Growing Tired of My Love   3:38   Spare
  Parts
- Antique Angelique 3:23   Spare Parts
- So Ends Another Life   3:11   Spare Parts
- Poor Old Man   3:37   Spare Parts
- Mr. Mind Detector 4:00   Spare Parts
- The Clown 3:24   Spare Parts
- Velvet Curtains   2:59   Spare Parts
- Little Miss Nothing 3:01   Spare Parts
- When I Awake   3:51   Spare Parts
- Nothing At All   3:53   Spare Parts
- Josie (Out-Take Version)   3:35   Spare Parts
- Do You Live In Fire (Stereo)   2:16   Spare Parts
- Face Without a Soul (Mono Version)   3:09   Spare
  Parts
- You're Just What I Was Looking for Today (Mono
  Version)   3:50   Spare Parts
- Are You Growing Tired of My Love (Mono)   3:38
  Spare Parts

- Antique Angelique (Mono Version)　　3:24　　Spare Parts
- So Ends Another Life (Mono Version)　　3:12　　Spare Parts
- Poor Old Man (Mono Version)　　3:40　　Spare Parts
- Mr. Mind Detector (Mono) 4:02　　Spare Parts
- The Clown (Mono Version)　　3:24　　Spare Parts
- Velvet Curtains (Mono)　　3:00　　Spare Parts
- Little Miss Nothing (Mono)　　3:02　　Spare Parts
- When I Awake (Mono Version)　　3:53　　Spare Parts
- Nothing At All (Mono Version)　　3:56　　Spare Parts
- Nothing At All (Part of Demo - Mono)　　2:22　　Spare Parts
- The Price of Love　3:40　　Spare Parts
- Pictures of Matchstick Men (Mono Version)　　3:14　　Down the Dustpipe
- Gentleman Joe's Sidewalk Cafe　　2:59　　Down the Dustpipe
- Black Veils of Melancholy (Mono Version) 3:13　　Down the Dustpipe
- To Be Free (Mono Version) 2:35　　Down the Dustpipe
- Ice in the Sun　　2:10　　Down the Dustpipe
- Elizabeth Dreams　　3:46　　Down the Dustpipe
- Paradise Flat　　3:13　　Down the Dustpipe
- Spicks and Specks　2:51　　Down the Dustpipe
- Sheila　　1:54　　Down the Dustpipe
- Sunny Cellophane Skies　　2:46　　Down the Dustpipe
- Green Tambourine 2:17　　Down the Dustpipe

- Make Me Stay a Little Bit Longer (A-Side Version) 2:53 Down the Dustpipe
- Auntie Nellie (B-Side Version)   3:30   Down the Dustpipe
- Are You Growing Tired of My Love (Mono Version) 3:36 Down the Dustpipe
- Face Without a Soul   3:07   Down the Dustpipe
- Down the Dustpipe 2:03   Down the Dustpipe
- Spinning Wheel Blues   3:18   Down the Dustpipe
- Daughter   3:00   Down the Dustpipe
- Everything 2:35   Down the Dustpipe
- Gerdundula 3:21   Down the Dustpipe
- Junior's Wailing   3:32   Down the Dustpipe
- Lakky Lady 3:12   Down the Dustpipe
- Need Your Love   4:44   Down the Dustpipe
- Lazy Poker Blues   3:35   Down the Dustpipe
- Is It Really Me / Gotta Go Home   9:29   Down the Dustpipe
- In My Chair 3:13   Down the Dustpipe
- Tune to the Music (7" Single Version)   3:06   Down the Dustpipe
- Good Thinking   3:40   Down the Dustpipe
- Something's Going on in My Head 4:43   Down the Dustpipe
- Mean Girl   3:53   Down the Dustpipe
- Spinning Wheel Blues   3:18   Ma Kelly's Greasy Spoon
- Daughter   3:01   Ma Kelly's Greasy Spoon

- Everything 2:35   Ma Kelly's Greasy Spoon
- Shy Fly   3:47   Ma Kelly's Greasy Spoon
- (April) Spring, Summer & Wednesdays   4:10   Ma Kelly's Greasy Spoon
- Junior's Wailing   3:32   Ma Kelly's Greasy Spoon
- Lakky Lady 3:12   Ma Kelly's Greasy Spoon
- Need Your Love   4:45   Ma Kelly's Greasy Spoon
- Lazy Poker Blues   3:35   Ma Kelly's Greasy Spoon
- Is It Really Me / Gotta Go Home   9:30   Ma Kelly's Greasy Spoon
- Is It Really Me / Gotta Go Home (Early Rough Mix) 6:52 Ma Kelly's Greasy Spoon
- Daughter (Early Working Mix)   2:55   Ma Kelly's Greasy Spoon
- Down the Dustpipe 2:03   Ma Kelly's Greasy Spoon
- In My Chair 3:17   Ma Kelly's Greasy Spoon
- Gerdundula (7" Version)   3:21   Ma Kelly's Greasy Spoon
- Down the Dustpipe (Live at the BBC)   1:49   Ma Kelly's Greasy Spoon
- Junior's Wailing (Live at the BBC) 2:58   Ma Kelly's Greasy Spoon
- Spinning Wheel Blues (Live at the BBC)   2:13   Ma Kelly's Greasy Spoon
- Need Your Love (Live at the BBC) 2:27   Ma Kelly's Greasy Spoon
- In My Chair (1979 Pye Promo Flexidisc)   1:37   Ma Kelly's Greasy Spoon

- Roll Over Lay Down   5:42   Hello
- Claudie   4:04   Hello
- Reason For Living   3:44   Hello
- Blue Eyed Lady   3:53   Hello
- Caroline   4:19   Hello
- Softer Ride 4:02   Hello
- And It's Better Now 3:20   Hello
- Forty-Five Hundred Times 9:54   Hello
- Joanne   4:07   Hello

Playlist: Status Quo 2

"In the Army Now" (2010)
Status Quo marches into the battlefield of rock with their iconic album, "In the Army Now." Released in 2010, this album showcases the band's enduring spirit and their ability to captivate audiences with their signature sound. With anthems like the title track "In the Army Now" and the infectious "Rollin' Home," Status Quo delivers a powerful collection of rock 'n' roll ammunition that strikes a chord with listeners. Prepare to be enlisted into a sonic journey that combines the band's unmistakable energy with a modern edge, leaving you ready to conquer any musical battlefield.

"Don't Stop: The 30th Anniversary Album"
Celebrating three decades of rock 'n' roll excellence, "Don't Stop: The 30th Anniversary Album" is a milestone in Status Quo's illustrious career. This compilation captures the band's iconic hits, showcasing their evolution and unwavering dedication to crafting infectious rock anthems. From the timeless classic "Rockin' All Over the World" to the foot-

stomping rhythms of "Whatever You Want," this album is a testament to Status Quo's ability to captivate audiences and ignite the flames of rock 'n' roll passion. Get ready to embark on a celebratory journey through three decades of unforgettable music.

"Heavy Traffic"

With their album "Heavy Traffic," Status Quo invites you to join them on a high-octane ride through the fast lanes of rock 'n' roll. Packed with electrifying riffs, pulsating rhythms, and the unmistakable vocals of Francis Rossi, this album delivers a relentless onslaught of pure musical horsepower. From the gritty energy of "Creepin' Up on You" to the infectious groove of "Jam Side Down," "Heavy Traffic" showcases Status Quo's ability to create hard-hitting, foot-stomping anthems that demand to be played at maximum volume. Buckle up, hit the gas pedal, and let the heavy traffic of rock 'n' roll consume you.

"Rockin' All Over the World"

Status Quo takes their infectious rock 'n' roll anthems to global proportions with "Rockin' All Over the World." This album encapsulates the band's ability to craft catchy hooks and electrifying rhythms that transcend borders and unite fans worldwide. From the stadium-sized title track to the rollicking energy of "Hold You Back," Status Quo's music becomes a unifying force that resonates with the spirit of rock lovers across the globe. "Rockin' All Over the World" is an invitation to join the party and embrace the universal language of music that transcends boundaries.

"The Party Ain't over Yet"
Status Quo proves that the party never ends with their album
"The Party Ain't over Yet." This collection of rock 'n' roll
gems encapsulates the band's unwavering spirit and their
ability to create music that defies time and age. From the
rebellious energy of the title track to the infectious groove of
"All That Counts Is Love," Status Quo invites you to immerse
yourself in an unrelenting celebration of life, music, and the
joy of letting loose. So crank up the volume, grab a drink, and
join the party that refuses to fade away.

"In Search of the Fourth Chord"
On a relentless quest for the ultimate chord progression,
Status Quo embarks on a musical odyssey with "In Search of
the Fourth Chord." This album is a testament to the band's
dedication to their craft and their unwavering commitment
to delivering rock 'n' roll excellence. From the thunderous
opening riff of "Beginning of the End" to the infectious
energy of "Electric Arena," Status Quo showcases their ability
to weave together irresistible melodies and timeless rock
sensibilities. Join the band on their sonic expedition as they
explore the uncharted territories of rock, in search of that
elusive fourth chord.

"Under the Influence" (1 Remastered Version)
Prepare to be under the intoxicating spell of Status Quo's
"Under the Influence" (1 Remastered Version). This album
pays homage to the band's own musical influences,
channeling their energy and spirit into a collection of
captivating tracks. From the gritty blues-rock of "Twenty
Wild Horses" to the infectious grooves of "Rock 'Til You
Drop," Status Quo serves up a potent cocktail of rock 'n' roll,
laced with their signature style and undeniable charisma. Get

ready to surrender yourself to the mesmerizing power of music and let the intoxicating influence of Status Quo wash over you.

"Quid Pro Quo"

Status Quo strikes a harmonious balance between their classic rock roots and their modern rock sensibilities with "Quid Pro Quo." This album is a testament to the band's ability to evolve while staying true to their signature sound. From the hard-hitting rhythms of "Two-Way Traffic" to the anthemic chorus of "Rock 'n' Roll 'n' You," Status Quo delivers an exhilarating sonic experience that seamlessly blends nostalgia with a contemporary edge. "Quid Pro Quo" is a musical exchange that rewards both the band and the listener with a collection of powerful, infectious rock 'n' roll.

"Aquostic II - That's a Fact!"

Status Quo unveils the acoustic side of their rock 'n' roll prowess with "Aquostic II - That's a Fact!" This album reimagines their classic hits in stripped-down acoustic arrangements, revealing the timeless beauty and raw emotion of the songs. From the heartfelt rendition of "In the Army Now" to the soulful intimacy of "Rain," Status Quo showcases their versatility and musical depth, proving that great songs can shine in any form. So sit back, let the acoustic melodies wash over you, and rediscover the magic of Status Quo in a whole new light.

"Backbone"

With their album "Backbone," Status Quo solidifies their status as rock legends. This release showcases the band's unwavering determination and their ability to create anthems that stand the test of time. From the thunderous opening track "Waiting for a Woman" to the infectious energy of "Liberty Lane," "Backbone" is a testament to the band's enduring spirit and their unrelenting commitment to the power of rock 'n' roll. Status Quo's distinctive sound, fueled by Francis Rossi and Rick Parfitt's iconic guitar interplay, remains the backbone of their music, delivering a collection of songs that resonate deep within the soul.

"Aquostic (Stripped Bare)" [Deluxe Version]
Prepare to experience the raw essence of Status Quo like never before with the "Aquostic (Stripped Bare)" [Deluxe Version]. Stripped of electric power but brimming with emotional intensity, this album showcases the band's classic hits in an acoustic setting that lays bare their musical brilliance. From the haunting beauty of "Down Down" to the intimate warmth of "Pictures of Matchstick Men," Status Quo reveals new layers of depth and vulnerability in their music, proving that even in their simplest form, their songs possess an undeniable power. Embrace the bare honesty of "Aquostic (Stripped Bare)" and rediscover the timeless magic of Status Quo..

- In the Army Now 2010   4:21   In the Army Now (2010)
- I Ain't Wasting My Time   3:37   In the Army Now (2010)
- One by One 4:13   In the Army Now (2010)
- In the Army Now (2010) [Radio Edit]   3:52   In the Army Now (2010)
- Fun Fun Fun (with the Beach Boys)   4:02   Don't Stop: The 30th Anniversary Album

- When You Walk in the Room 4:07 Don't Stop: The 30th Anniversary Album
- I Can Hear the Grass Grow 3:24 Don't Stop: The 30th Anniversary Album
- You Never Can Tell (It Was a Teenage Wedding) 3:51 Don't Stop: The 30th Anniversary Album
- Get Back 3:23 Don't Stop: The 30th Anniversary Album
- Safety Dance 3:56 Don't Stop: The 30th Anniversary Album
- Raining in My Heart (with Brian May) 3:33 Don't Stop: The 30th Anniversary Album
- Don't Stop 3:39 Don't Stop: The 30th Anniversary Album
- Sorrow 4:14 Don't Stop: The 30th Anniversary Album
- Proud Mary 3:31 Don't Stop: The 30th Anniversary Album
- Lucille 2:58 Don't Stop: The 30th Anniversary Album
- Johnny and Mary 3:35 Don't Stop: The 30th Anniversary Album
- Get out of Denver 4:09 Don't Stop: The 30th Anniversary Album
- The Future's so Bright (I Gotta Wear Shades) 3:36 Don't Stop: The 30th Anniversary Album
- All Around My Hat (with Maddy Prior) 3:56 Don't Stop: The 30th Anniversary Album
- Blues and Rhythm 4:29 Heavy Traffic
- All Stand Up (Never Say Never) 4:08 Heavy Traffic
- The Oriental 4:29 Heavy Traffic
- Creepin Up on You 5:01 Heavy Traffic
- Heavy Traffic 4:23 Heavy Traffic

- Solid Gold   4:12   Heavy Traffic
- Green   3:35   Heavy Traffic
- Jam Side Down   3:27   Heavy Traffic
- Diggin' Burt Bacharach   2:32   Heavy Traffic
- Do It Again 3:39   Heavy Traffic
- Another Day   3:47   Heavy Traffic
- I Don't Remember Anymore   3:38   Heavy Traffic
- Rhythm of Life   5:05   Heavy Traffic
- Hard Time   4:45   Rockin' All Over the World
- Can't Give You More   4:17   Rockin' All Over the World
- Let's Ride   3:04   Rockin' All Over the World
- Baby Boy   3:13   Rockin' All Over the World
- You Don't Own Me 3:04   Rockin' All Over the World
- Rockers Rollin'   4:18   Rockin' All Over the World
- Rockin' All Over the World3:37   Rockin' All Over the World
- Who Am I? 4:31   Rockin' All Over the World
- Too Far Gone   3:08   Rockin' All Over the World
- For You   3:01   Rockin' All Over the World
- Dirty Water 3:52   Rockin' All Over the World
- Hold You Back   4:31   Rockin' All Over the World
- Getting Better   2:22   Rockin' All Over the World
- The Party Ain't over Yet (Single Mix)   3:51   The Party Ain't over Yet (Bonus Tracks)
- Belavista Man (Live in Emden)   4:34   The Party Ain't over Yet (Bonus Tracks)
- I'm Not Ready   4:33   The Party Ain't over Yet (Bonus Tracks)
- I'm Watching over You   3:49   The Party Ain't over Yet (Bonus Tracks)
- The Party Ain't over Yet   3:50   The Party Ain't over Yet

- Gotta Get up and Go 4:18 The Party Ain't over Yet
- All That Counts Is Love 3:41 The Party Ain't over Yet
- Familiar Blues 5:09 The Party Ain't over Yet
- The Bubble 5:36 The Party Ain't over Yet
- Belavista Man 4:21 The Party Ain't over Yet
- Nevashooda 3:52 The Party Ain't over Yet
- Velvet Train 3:33 The Party Ain't over Yet
- Goodbye Baby 4:08 The Party Ain't over Yet
- You Never Stop 4:33 The Party Ain't over Yet
- Kick Me When I'm Down 3:17 The Party Ain't over Yet
- Cupid Stupid 3:51 The Party Ain't over Yet
- This Is Me 4:47 The Party Ain't over Yet
- Beginning of the End 4:29 In Search of the Fourth Chord
- Alright 4:12 In Search of the Fourth Chord
- Pennsylvania Blues Tonight 3:41 In Search of the Fourth Chord
- I Don't Wanna Hurt You Anymore 3:59 In Search of the Fourth Chord
- Electric Arena 5:22 In Search of the Fourth Chord
- Gravy Train 3:23 In Search of the Fourth Chord
- Figure of Eight 4:07 In Search of the Fourth Chord
- You're the One for Me 3:31 In Search of the Fourth Chord
- My Little Heartbreaker 3:50 In Search of the Fourth Chord
- Hold Me 4:34 In Search of the Fourth Chord
- Saddling Up 3:41 In Search of the Fourth Chord
- Bad News 5:05 In Search of the Fourth Chord
- Tongue Tied 4:24 In Search of the Fourth Chord

- One By One 4:13   In Search of the Fourth Chord
- Twenty Wild Horses (Remastered Version)5:00   Under the Influence (1 Remastered Version)
- Under the Influence (Remastered Version) 4:05   Under the Influence (1 Remastered Version)
- Round and Round (Remastered Version)   3:25   Under the Influence (1 Remastered Version)
- Shine On (Remastered Version)   4:47   Under the Influence (1 Remastered Version)
- Little White Lies (Remastered Version)   4:20   Under the Influence (1 Remastered Version)
- Keep 'Em Coming (Remastered Version)   3:27   Under the Influence (1 Remastered Version)
- Little Me and You (Remastered Version)   3:49   Under the Influence (1 Remastered Version)
- Making Waves (Remastered Version)   3:59   Under the Influence (1 Remastered Version)
- Blessed Are the Meek (Remastered Version)   4:22   Under the Influence (1 Remastered Version)
- Roll the Dice (Remastered Version)4:06   Under the Influence (1 Remastered Version)
- Not Fade Away (Remastered Version)   3:11   Under the Influence (1 Remastered Version)
- The Way It Goes (Remastered Version)   4:02   Under the Influence (1 Remastered Version)
- Sea Cruise (Bonus Track)   3:12   Under the Influence (1 Remastered Version)
- I Knew the Bride (Bonus Track)   3:35   Under the Influence (1 Remastered Version)
- Twenty Wild Horses (Bonus Track) [Live] 4:53   Under the Influence (1 Remastered Version)
- Pictures of Matchstick Men (1999 Version) 3:22   Under the Influence (1 Remastered Version)

- Two Way Traffic 3:59 Quid Pro Quo
- Rock 'n' Roll 'n' You3:27 Quid Pro Quo
- Dust to Gold 4:51 Quid Pro Quo
- Let's Rock 4:27 Quid Pro Quo
- Can't See for Looking 3:54 Quid Pro Quo
- Better Than That 3:17 Quid Pro Quo
- Movin' On 4:06 Quid Pro Quo
- Leave a Little Light On 4:04 Quid Pro Quo
- Any Way You Like It 3:17 Quid Pro Quo
- Frozen Hero 4:20 Quid Pro Quo
- Reality Cheque 4:05 Quid Pro Quo
- The Winner 3:17 Quid Pro Quo
- It's All About You 2:53 Quid Pro Quo
- My Old Ways 3:04 Quid Pro Quo
- In the Army Now (2010) 4:21 Quid Pro Quo
- That's a Fact 3:35 Aquostic Ii-That's a Fact!
- Roll over Lay Down 4:28 Aquostic Ii-That's a Fact!
- Dear John 3:28 Aquostic Ii-That's a Fact!
- In the Army Now 4:03 Aquostic Ii-That's a Fact!
- Hold You Back 4:10 Aquostic Ii-That's a Fact!
- One for the Road 3:33 Aquostic Ii-That's a Fact!
- Backwater 4:52 Aquostic Ii-That's a Fact!
- One of Everything 3:47 Aquostic Ii-That's a Fact!
- Belavista Man 3:52 Aquostic Ii-That's a Fact!
- Lover of the Human Race 3:44 Aquostic Ii-That's a Fact!
- Ice in the Sun 2:20 Aquostic Ii-That's a Fact!
- Mess of the Blues 2:32 Aquostic Ii-That's a Fact!
- Jam Side Down 3:12 Aquostic Ii-That's a Fact!
- Resurrection 3:12 Aquostic Ii-That's a Fact!
- Waiting for a Woman 4:27 Backbone
- Cut Me Some Slack 4:21 Backbone

- Liberty Lane   3:42   Backbone
- I See You're in Some Trouble   3:46   Backbone
- Backing Off 4:11   Backbone
- I Wanna Run Away with You   3:23   Backbone
- Backbone   3:03   Backbone
- Better Take Care   3:34   Backbone
- Falling off the World   3:28   Backbone
- Get out of My Head 3:24   Backbone
- Running out of Time   3:28   Backbone
- Pictures of Matchstick Men 3:37   Aquostic (Stripped Bare) [Deluxe Version]
- Down the Dustpipe 2:40   Aquostic (Stripped Bare) [Deluxe Version]
- Nanana   2:55   Aquostic (Stripped Bare) [Deluxe Version]
- Paper Plane 3:37   Aquostic (Stripped Bare) [Deluxe Version]
- All the Reasons   3:07   Aquostic (Stripped Bare) [Deluxe Version]
- Reason for Living   3:20   Aquostic (Stripped Bare) [Deluxe Version]
- And It's Better Now 3:41   Aquostic (Stripped Bare) [Deluxe Version]
- Caroline   3:12   Aquostic (Stripped Bare) [Deluxe Version]
- Softer Ride 2:56   Aquostic (Stripped Bare) [Deluxe Version]
- Claudie   3:57   Aquostic (Stripped Bare) [Deluxe Version]
- Break the Rules   3:09   Aquostic (Stripped Bare) [Deluxe Version]
- Down Down   2:36   Aquostic (Stripped Bare) [Deluxe Version]

- Rain 3:56   Aquostic (Stripped Bare) [Deluxe Version]
- Rockin' All over the World 2:40   Aquostic (Stripped Bare) [Deluxe Version]
- Again and Again   3:20   Aquostic (Stripped Bare) [Deluxe Version]
- Whatever You Want   3:25   Aquostic (Stripped Bare) [Deluxe Version]
- What You're Proposing   2:04   Aquostic (Stripped Bare) [Deluxe Version]
- Rock 'N' Roll   2:42   Aquostic (Stripped Bare) [Deluxe Version]
- Don't Drive My Car 3:10   Aquostic (Stripped Bare) [Deluxe Version]
- Marguerita Time   3:19   Aquostic (Stripped Bare) [Deluxe Version]
- Rollin' Home (Bonus Track)   4:05   Aquostic (Stripped Bare) [Deluxe Version]
- Burning Bridges   3:45   Aquostic (Stripped Bare) [Deluxe Version]
- Rock 'Til You Drop 2:48   Aquostic (Stripped Bare) [Deluxe Version]

Playlist: Status Quo 3

"Status Quo Live"
Get ready to witness the raw power and infectious energy of Status Quo in their element with "Status Quo Live." This album captures the band's electrifying stage presence and their ability to ignite crowds with their signature rock 'n' roll anthems. From the thunderous opening chords of "Caroline" to the foot-stomping frenzy of "Rockin' All Over the World," Status Quo delivers a live experience that transports you to the front row of a legendary concert. Feel the adrenaline rush and let the music take hold as you become part of the roaring crowd, experiencing the unstoppable force of Status Quo in their prime.

"The Last Night of the Electrics"
Prepare for a night of electrifying rock 'n' roll as Status Quo bids farewell to their electric era with "The Last Night of the Electrics." Recorded live, this album captures the band's final explosive performance before embracing a new acoustic direction. From the high-voltage energy of "Whatever You

Want" to the timeless anthem "Rockin' All Over the World," Status Quo unleashes a sonic onslaught that encapsulates the power and passion that defined their electrifying journey. Join them on this unforgettable farewell and witness the sparks fly as the curtains close on an era of rock history.

"Down Down & Dirty at Wacken"
Status Quo unleashes a fierce and gritty performance at the iconic Wacken Open Air festival with "Down Down & Dirty at Wacken." Recorded live, this album captures the band's unrelenting energy and their ability to ignite massive crowds. From the thunderous riffage of "Roll Over Lay Down" to the adrenaline-fueled intensity of "Down Down," Status Quo delivers a setlist that leaves no fan unsatisfied. It's a headbanging, fist-pumping experience that immerses you in the raw power of their rock 'n' roll onslaught. Prepare to get down, get dirty, and rock out at the legendary Wacken festival.

"Down Down & Dignified at the Royal Albert Hall" (Live)
Status Quo trades their raucous electric guitars for acoustic elegance in a majestic performance at the Royal Albert Hall with "Down Down & Dignified at the Royal Albert Hall." This live album showcases the band's versatility and musical prowess as they reimagine their hits in stripped-down, intimate arrangements. From the soulful rendition of "In the Army Now" to the delicate beauty of "Caroline," Status Quo proves that their songs can resonate just as powerfully in a more dignified setting. Let the grandeur of the Royal Albert Hall envelop you as you witness the band's acoustic brilliance in this unforgettable live performance.

"Aquostic! Live at the Roundhouse"
Status Quo's "Aquostic! Live at the Roundhouse" is a testament to the band's ability to captivate audiences with their acoustic reinvention. Recorded live at the iconic Roundhouse, this album showcases the band's stripped-down renditions of their classic hits. From the heartfelt beauty of "Pictures of Matchstick Men" to the foot-tapping energy of "Rock 'n' Roll 'n' You," Status Quo infuses their songs with a newfound depth and intimacy. Experience the magic of their acoustic journey as they breathe new life into their beloved catalog, creating an enchanting atmosphere that leaves a lasting impression.

"The Frantic Four's Final Fling - Live at the Dublin O2 Arena"
Witness a historic moment in rock 'n' roll history with "The Frantic Four's Final Fling - Live at the Dublin O2 Arena." This album captures the reunion of the original Frantic Four lineup, as Francis Rossi, Rick Parfitt, Alan Lancaster, and John Coghlan take the stage for one last explosive performance. From the blistering intensity of "Down the Dustpipe" to the iconic riffs of "Caroline," the Frantic Four reignite the flame of their youthful energy, transporting fans back to the golden era of Status Quo. Experience the power, the nostalgia, and the unmatched chemistry of the Frantic Four as they bid farewell in unforgettable fashion.

"Back2sq1: The Frantic Four Reunion 2013 (Live at Hammersmith)"
Relive the glory days of Status Quo as the legendary Frantic Four lineup reunites for an unforgettable performance at Hammersmith with "Back2sq1: The Frantic Four Reunion 2013." This live album captures the magic and raw energy of

the band's original lineup as they revisit their iconic hits. From the thunderous riffage of "Junior's Wailing" to the rebellious spirit of "Down the Dustpipe," the Frantic Four reignites the flame of their early days, transporting fans back to the birth of British boogie rock. Join the celebration and experience the sheer power and unbridled joy of the Frantic Four reunion.

"In the Army Now" (2010)

Status Quo takes their signature hits to the stage with "In the Army Now" (2010). This live album captures the band's electrifying performances as they breathe new life into their iconic songs. From the anthemic title track "In the Army Now" to the crowd-pleasing energy of "Roll Over Lay Down," Status Quo showcases their ability to deliver a high-octane, rock 'n' roll experience that leaves audiences craving for more. Immerse yourself in the excitement and let the power of live music surround you as Status Quo marches forward, armed with their timeless hits.

"The Party Ain't over Yet" (Bonus Tracks)

Continue the party with "The Party Ain't over Yet" (Bonus Tracks) from Status Quo. This live album features additional tracks that were not included in the original release, bringing more of the band's high-energy performances to the forefront. From the infectious grooves of "All Stand Up (Never Say Never)" to the rebellious spirit of "Rock 'n' Me," Status Quo keeps the celebration going with their unrelenting rock 'n' roll spirit. These bonus tracks are a perfect addition to the original album, ensuring that the party never stops and the joy of Status Quo's music resonates even stronger.

- Junior's Wailing (Live)   5:21   Status Quo Live
- Backwater / Just Take Me (Live At Glasgow Apollo, Glasgow / 1976)   8:27   Status Quo Live
- Is There a Better Way (Live At Glasgow Apollo, Glasgow / 1976)   4:17   Status Quo Live
- In My Chair (Live At Glasgow Apollo, Glasgow / 1976) 3:34 Status Quo Live
- Little Lady / Most of the Time (Live At Glasgow Apollo, Glasgow / 1976)   7:06   Status Quo Live
- Forty-Five Hundred Times (Live At Glasgow Apollo, Glasgow / 1976)   16:53   Status Quo Live
- Roll Over Lay Down (Live At Glasgow Apollo, Glasgow / 1976)   6:05   Status Quo Live
- Big Fat Mama (Live At Glasgow Apollo, Glasgow / 1976) 5:13 Status Quo Live
- Caroline (Live At Glasgow Apollo, Glasgow / 1976) 6:40 Status Quo Live
- Bye Bye Johnny (Live At Glasgow Apollo, Glasgow / 1976) 6:24 Status Quo Live
- Rain (Live At Glasgow Apollo, Glasgow / 1976)   4:57 Status Quo Live
- Don't Waste My Time (Live At Glasgow Apollo, Glasgow / 1976)   4:04   Status Quo Live
- Roadhouse Blues (Live At Glasgow Apollo, Glasgow / 1976)   14:23   Status Quo Live
- Is There a Better Way (Live At Sunplaza Hall, Japan / 1976)   4:01   Status Quo Live
- Little Lady (Live At Sunplaza Hall, Japan / 1976)   3:03 Status Quo Live
- Most of the Time (Live At Sunplaza Hall, Japan / 1976) 3:37 Status Quo Live

- Rain (Live At Sunplaza Hall, Japan / 1976) 4:36   Status Quo Live
- Caroline (Live At Sunplaza Hall, Japan / 1976)   4:29 Status Quo Live
- Roll Over Lay Down (Live At Sunplaza Hall, Japan / 1976) 6:08 Status Quo Live
- Big Fat Mama (Live At Sunplaza Hall, Japan / 1976) 5:15 Status Quo Live
- Don't Waste My Time (Live At Sunplaza Hall, Japan / 1976)   4:14   Status Quo Live
- Bye Bye Johnny (Live At Sunplaza Hall, Japan / 1976) 6:58 Status Quo Live
- Junior's Wailing (Live At Hordern Pavilion, Sydney, Australia / 1974)   4:04   Status Quo Live
- Backwater (Live At Hordern Pavilion, Sydney, Australia / 1974)   4:37   Status Quo Live
- Just Take Me (Live At Hordern Pavilion, Sydney, Australia / 1974)   3:47   Status Quo Live
- Claudie (Live At Hordern Pavilion, Sydney, Australia / 1974)   4:18   Status Quo Live
- Railroad (Live At Hordern Pavilion, Sydney, Australia / 1974)   5:51   Status Quo Live
- Roll Over Lay Down (Live At Hordern Pavilion, Sydney, Australia / 1974)   5:39   Status Quo Live
- Big Fat Mama (Live At Hordern Pavilion, Sydney, Australia / 1974)   5:24   Status Quo Live
- Don't Waste My Time (Live At Hordern Pavilion, Sydney, Australia / 1974)   4:14   Status Quo Live
- Roadhouse Blues (Pt. 1/ Live At Hordern Pavilion, Sydney, Australia / 1974)   8:54   Status Quo Live
- Roadhouse Blues (Pt. 2/ Live At Hordern Pavilion, Sydney, Australia / 1974)   1:37   Status Quo Live

- Caroline (Live At Hordern Pavilion, Sydney, Australia / 1974)   4:16   Status Quo Live
- Drum Solo (Live At Hordern Pavilion, Sydney, Australia / 1974)   3:20   Status Quo Live
- Bye Bye Johnny (Live At Hordern Pavilion, Sydney, Australia / 1974)   6:14   Status Quo Live
- Caroline (Live in London 2016)   5:27   The Last Night of the Electrics
- The Wanderer (Live in London 2016)   2:45   The Last Night of the Electrics
- Something 'Bout You Baby I Like (Live in London 2016) 2:17 The Last Night of the Electrics
- Rain (Live in London 2016) 4:35   The Last Night of the Electrics
- Softer Ride (Live in London 2016) 4:02   The Last Night of the Electrics
- Beginning of the End (Live in London 2016)   3:57 The Last Night of the Electrics
- Hold You Back (Live in London 2016)   4:45   The Last Night of the Electrics
- Proposing Medley (Live in London 2016) 7:25   The Last Night of the Electrics
- Paper Plane (Live in London 2016) 3:30   The Last Night of the Electrics
- The Oriental (Live in London 2016)   5:14   The Last Night of the Electrics
- Creepin' up on You (Live in London 2016) 4:58   The Last Night of the Electrics
- Gerdundula (Live in London 2016) 5:02   The Last Night of the Electrics
- In the Army Now (Live in London 2016)   4:08   The Last Night of the Electrics

- Drum Solo (The Caveman) [Live in London 2016] 3:10 The Last Night of the Electrics
- Roll over Lay Down (Live in London 2016)   5:58 The Last Night of the Electrics
- Down Down (Live in London 2016)   7:17   The Last Night of the Electrics
- Whatever You Want (Live in London 2016)   5:03 The Last Night of the Electrics
- Rockin' All over the World (Live in London 2016) 4:03 The Last Night of the Electrics
- Burning Bridges (Live in London 2016)   3:52   The Last Night of the Electrics
- Rock 'N' Roll / Bye Bye Johnny (Live in London 2016) 6:29 The Last Night of the Electrics
- Caroline (Live at Wacken 2017)   5:31   Down Down & Dirty at Wacken
- Something About You Baby I Like (Live at Wacken 2017) 2:16 Down Down & Dirty at Wacken
- Rain (Live at Wacken 2017) 5:01   Down Down & Dirty at Wacken
- Softer Ride (Live at Wacken 2017) 4:02   Down Down & Dirty at Wacken
- Beginning of the End (Live at Wacken 2017)   3:54 Down Down & Dirty at Wacken
- Hold You Back (Live at Wacken 2017)   5:09   Down Down & Dirty at Wacken
- Proposin' Medley (Live at Wacken 2017)   7:24   Down Down & Dirty at Wacken
- Paper Plane (Live at Wacken 2017) 3:39   Down Down & Dirty at Wacken
- In the Army Now (Live at Wacken 2017)   4:14   Down Down & Dirty at Wacken

- Roll over Lay Down (Live at Wacken 2017)   5:52
  Down Down & Dirty at Wacken
- Down Down (Live at Wacken 2017)   6:36   Down
  Down & Dirty at Wacken
- Whatever You Want (Live at Wacken 2017)   5:01
  Down Down & Dirty at Wacken
- Rockin' All over the World (Live at Wacken 2017) 4:53
  Down Down & Dirty at Wacken
- Rock and Roll Music/Bye Bye Johnny (Live at Wacken
  2017)   7:33   Down Down & Dirty at Wacken
- And It's Better Now (Live at the Royal Albert Hall 2017)
  4:08 Down Down & Dignified at the Royal Albert Hall
  (Live)
- Break the Rules (Live at the Royal Albert Hall 2017)
  3:09 Down Down & Dignified at the Royal Albert Hall
  (Live)
- Again and Again (Live at the Royal Albert Hall 2017)
  3:24 Down Down & Dignified at the Royal Albert Hall
  (Live)
- Paper Plane (Live at the Royal Albert Hall 2017)   3:47
  Down Down & Dignified at the Royal Albert Hall (Live)
- Rock 'n' Roll (Live at the Royal Albert Hall 2017)   3:06
  Down Down & Dignified at the Royal Albert Hall (Live)
- Caroline (Live at the Royal Albert Hall 2017)   3:15
  Down Down & Dignified at the Royal Albert Hall (Live)
- What You're Proposing (Live at the Royal Albert Hall
  2017)   2:10   Down Down & Dignified at the Royal
  Albert Hall (Live)
- Hold You Back (Live at the Royal Albert Hall 2017) 4:19
  Down Down & Dignified at the Royal Albert Hall (Live)
- That's a Fact (Live at the Royal Albert Hall 2017)   3:50
  Down Down & Dignified at the Royal Albert Hall (Live)

- Down Down (Live at the Royal Albert Hall 2017) 2:42 Down Down & Dignified at the Royal Albert Hall (Live)
- Pictures of Matchstick Men (Live at the Royal Albert Hall 2017)   3:18   Down Down & Dignified at the Royal Albert Hall (Live)
- Down the Dustpipe (Live at the Royal Albert Hall 2017) 2:38 Down Down & Dignified at the Royal Albert Hall (Live)
- All the Reasons (Live at the Royal Albert Hall 2017) 3:10 Down Down & Dignified at the Royal Albert Hall (Live)
- Rollin' Home (Live at the Royal Albert Hall 2017) 4:12 Down Down & Dignified at the Royal Albert Hall (Live)
- Band Introductions (Live at the Royal Albert Hall 2017) 1:46 Down Down & Dignified at the Royal Albert Hall (Live)
- Don't Drive My Car (Live at the Royal Albert Hall 2017) 3:19 Down Down & Dignified at the Royal Albert Hall (Live)
- Reason for Living (Live at the Royal Albert Hall 2017) 3:20 Down Down & Dignified at the Royal Albert Hall (Live)
- Claudie (Live at the Royal Albert Hall 2017)   4:00 Down Down & Dignified at the Royal Albert Hall (Live)
- Rain (Live at the Royal Albert Hall 2017) 4:17   Down Down & Dignified at the Royal Albert Hall (Live)
- Marguerita Time (Live at the Royal Albert Hall 2017) 3:23 Down Down & Dignified at the Royal Albert Hall (Live)
- Na Na Na (Live at the Royal Albert Hall 2017)   2:57 Down Down & Dignified at the Royal Albert Hall (Live)

- Whatever You Want (Live at the Royal Albert Hall 2017) 3:20 Down Down & Dignified at the Royal Albert Hall (Live)
- Rockin' All over the World (Live at the Royal Albert Hall 2017)   3:31   Down Down & Dignified at the Royal Albert Hall (Live)
- Burning Bridges (Live at the Royal Albert Hall 2017) 4:21 Down Down & Dignified at the Royal Albert Hall (Live)
- And It's Better Now (Live & Acoustic)   4:26 Aquostic! Live at the Roundhouse
- Break the Rules (Live & Acoustic) 3:09   Aquostic! Live at the Roundhouse
- Again and Again (Live & Acoustic) 3:23   Aquostic! Live at the Roundhouse
- Paper Plane (Live & Acoustic)   5:11   Aquostic! Live at the Roundhouse
- Mystery Song (Live & Acoustic)   2:28   Aquostic! Live at the Roundhouse
- Little Lady (Live & Acoustic)   1:57   Aquostic! Live at the Roundhouse
- Rock 'N' Roll (Live & Acoustic)   2:41   Aquostic! Live at the Roundhouse
- Caroline (Live & Acoustic) 3:16   Aquostic! Live at the Roundhouse
- What You're Proposing (Live & Acoustic) 2:01 Aquostic! Live at the Roundhouse
- Softer Ride (Live & Acoustic)   4:25   Aquostic! Live at the Roundhouse
- Down Down (Live & Acoustic)   2:42   Aquostic! Live at the Roundhouse
- Pictures of Matchstick Men (Live & Acoustic)   3:47 Aquostic! Live at the Roundhouse

- Down the Dustpipe (Live & Acoustic)   2:49
  Aquostic! Live at the Roundhouse
- All the Reasons (Live & Acoustic)   3:12   Aquostic! Live
  at the Roundhouse
- Reason for Living (Live & Acoustic)   3:20
  Aquostic! Live at the Roundhouse
- Rollin' Home (Live & Acoustic)   4:59   Aquostic! Live
  at the Roundhouse
- Don't Drive My Car (Live & Acoustic)   3:21
  Aquostic! Live at the Roundhouse
- Claudie (Live & Acoustic)   4:05   Aquostic! Live at the
  Roundhouse
- Rain (Live & Acoustic)   3:59   Aquostic! Live at the
  Roundhouse
- Marguerita Time (Live & Acoustic) 3:23   Aquostic! Live
  at the Roundhouse
- Na Na Na (Live & Acoustic) 2:56   Aquostic! Live at the
  Roundhouse
- Whatever You Want (Live & Acoustic)   3:37
  Aquostic! Live at the Roundhouse
- Rockin ' All over the World (Live & Acoustic)   3:37
  Aquostic! Live at the Roundhouse
- Rock 'Til You Drop (Live & Acoustic)   2:54
  Aquostic! Live at the Roundhouse
- Burning Bridges (Live & Acoustic)   4:25   Aquostic! Live
  at the Roundhouse
- Junior's Wailing (Live in Dublin 2014)   4:19   The
  Frantic Four's Final Fling - Live at the Dublin O2 Arena
- Backwater (Live in Dublin 2014)   4:20   The Frantic
  Four's Final Fling - Live at the Dublin O2 Arena
- Just Take Me (Live in Dublin 2014) 3:31   The Frantic
  Four's Final Fling - Live at the Dublin O2 Arena

- Is There a Better Way (Live in Dublin 2014) 3:43 The Frantic Four's Final Fling - Live at the Dublin O2 Arena
- Blue Eyed Lady (Live in Dublin 2014) 3:51 The Frantic Four's Final Fling - Live at the Dublin O2 Arena
- In My Chair (Live in Dublin 2014) 3:12 The Frantic Four's Final Fling - Live at the Dublin O2 Arena
- Little Lady (Live in Dublin 2014) 3:18 The Frantic Four's Final Fling - Live at the Dublin O2 Arena
- Most of the Time (Live in Dublin 2014) 3:28 The Frantic Four's Final Fling - Live at the Dublin O2 Arena
- Rain (Live in Dublin 2014) 5:10 The Frantic Four's Final Fling - Live at the Dublin O2 Arena
- (April) Spring, Summer and Wednesdays (Live in Dublin 2014) 4:05 The Frantic Four's Final Fling - Live at the Dublin O2 Arena
- Railroad (Live in Dublin 2014) 5:50 The Frantic Four's Final Fling - Live at the Dublin O2 Arena
- Oh Baby (Live in Dublin 2014) 4:12 The Frantic Four's Final Fling - Live at the Dublin O2 Arena
- Forty - Five Hundred Times (Live in Dublin 2014) 6:21 The Frantic Four's Final Fling - Live at the Dublin O2 Arena
- Gotta Go Home (Live in Dublin 2014) 1:38 The Frantic Four's Final Fling - Live at the Dublin O2 Arena
- Big Fat Mama (Live in Dublin 2014) 5:31 The Frantic Four's Final Fling - Live at the Dublin O2 Arena
- Down Down (Live in Dublin 2014) 6:24 The Frantic Four's Final Fling - Live at the Dublin O2 Arena
- Roadhouse Blues (Live in Dublin 2014) 7:52 The Frantic Four's Final Fling - Live at the Dublin O2 Arena
- Caroline (Live in Dublin 2014) 4:25 The Frantic Four's Final Fling - Live at the Dublin O2 Arena

- Bye Bye Johnny (Live in Dublin 2014)   5:59   The Frantic Four's Final Fling - Live at the Dublin O2 Arena
- Intro / Junior's Wailing (Live at Hammersmith Apollo, London 15th-16th, March 2013)   4:21   Back2sq1: The Frantic Four Reunion 2013 (Live at Hammersmith)
- Backwater (Live at Hammersmith Apollo, London 15th-16th, March 2013)   4:20   Back2sq1: The Frantic Four Reunion 2013 (Live at Hammersmith)
- Just Take Me (Live at Hammersmith Apollo, London 15th-16th, March 2013)   4:56   Back2sq1: The Frantic Four Reunion 2013 (Live at Hammersmith)
- Is There a Better Way (Live at Hammersmith Apollo, London 15th-16th, March 2013)   3:47   Back2sq1: The Frantic Four Reunion 2013 (Live at Hammersmith)
- In My Chair (Live at Hammersmith Apollo, London 15th-16th, March 2013)   3:13   Back2sq1: The Frantic Four Reunion 2013 (Live at Hammersmith)
- Blue Eyed Lady (Live at Hammersmith Apollo, London 15th-16th, March 2013)   3:47   Back2sq1: The Frantic Four Reunion 2013 (Live at Hammersmith)
- Little Lady (Live at Hammersmith Apollo, London 15th-16th, March 2013)   3:14   Back2sq1: The Frantic Four Reunion 2013 (Live at Hammersmith)
- Most of the Time (Live at Hammersmith Apollo, London 15th-16th, March 2013)   3:19   Back2sq1: The Frantic Four Reunion 2013 (Live at Hammersmith)
- (April) Spring, Summer and Wednesdays (Live at Hammersmith Apollo, London 15th-16th, March 2013) 4:13 Back2sq1: The Frantic Four Reunion 2013 (Live at Hammersmith)
- Railroad (Live at Hammersmith Apollo, London 15th-16th, March 2013)   5:51   Back2sq1: The Frantic Four Reunion 2013 (Live at Hammersmith)

- Oh Baby (Live at Hammersmith Apollo, London 15th-16th, March 2013) 4:49 Back2sq1: The Frantic Four Reunion 2013 (Live at Hammersmith)
- Forty - Five Hundred Times (Live at Hammersmith Apollo, London 15th-16th, March 2013) 5:13 Back2sq1: The Frantic Four Reunion 2013 (Live at Hammersmith)
- Rain (Live at Hammersmith Apollo, London 15th-16th, March 2013) 5:04 Back2sq1: The Frantic Four Reunion 2013 (Live at Hammersmith)
- Big Fat Mama (Live at Hammersmith Apollo, London 15th-16th, March 2013) 5:27 Back2sq1: The Frantic Four Reunion 2013 (Live at Hammersmith)
- Down Down (Live at Hammersmith Apollo, London 15th-16th, March 2013) 5:57 Back2sq1: The Frantic Four Reunion 2013 (Live at Hammersmith)
- Roadhouse Blues (Live at Hammersmith Apollo, London 15th-16th, March 2013) 6:48 Back2sq1: The Frantic Four Reunion 2013 (Live at Hammersmith)
- Don't Waste My Time (Live at Hammersmith Apollo, London 15th-16th, March 2013) 4:27 Back2sq1: The Frantic Four Reunion 2013 (Live at Hammersmith)
- Bye Bye Johnny (Live at Hammersmith Apollo, London 15th-16th, March 2013) 6:41 Back2sq1: The Frantic Four Reunion 2013 (Live at Hammersmith)
- Rockin' All Over the World (Live at Live Aid, Wembley Stadium, 13th July 1985) 4:00 Status Quo at Live Aid (Live at Live Aid, Wembley Stadium, 13th July 1985) - Single
- Caroline (Live at Live Aid, Wembley Stadium, 13th July 1985) 4:34 Status Quo at Live Aid (Live at Live Aid, Wembley Stadium, 13th July 1985) - Single

- Don't Waste My Time (Live at Live Aid, Wembley Stadium, 13th July 1985)   4:45   Status Quo at Live Aid (Live at Live Aid, Wembley Stadium, 13th July 1985) - Single
- Caroline (Live from Ipswich Regent Theatre 17/02/09) 5:18 In the Army Now (2010)
- Beginning of the End (Live from Ipswich Regent Theatre 17/02/09)   4:22   In the Army Now (2010)
- Down Down (Live from Oxford New Theatre 04/10/08) 6:01 In the Army Now (2010)
- Burning Bridges (Live from Birmingham Mec 22/12/08) 3:50 In the Army Now (2010)
- Gerdundula (Live 2005)   6:49   The Party Ain't over Yet (Bonus Tracks)
- Live Medley (Mystery Song/Railroad/Most of the Time/ Wild Side of Life/Rollin' Home/Again and Again/Slow Train)   10:06   The Party Ain't over Yet (Bonus Tracks)

Ten Years After

Ten Years After is a British rock band that rose to
prominence during the late 1960s and early 1970s, known for
their electrifying blues-rock sound and captivating live
performances. The band was formed in Nottingham,
England, in 1966, and quickly gained recognition for their
energetic style and the virtuosic guitar playing of Alvin Lee.

The original lineup of Ten Years After consisted of Alvin Lee
on vocals and guitar, Leo Lyons on bass, Ric Lee on drums,
and Chick Churchill on keyboards. Drawing inspiration from

blues icons like Muddy Waters and Howlin' Wolf, the band added their own twist to the genre, infusing it with elements of rock and psychedelia.

Their breakthrough came in 1969 with the release of their second album, "Undead." The album included a captivating live performance of their song "I'm Going Home" at the Woodstock Festival, which showcased Alvin Lee's lightning-fast guitar work and instantly garnered the band widespread attention. This live performance became one of the defining moments of their career and solidified their reputation as a formidable live act.

Following the success of "Undead," Ten Years After continued to release a string of acclaimed albums throughout the early 1970s. Their 1970 album, "Cricklewood Green," featured the hit single "Love Like a Man" and further showcased their blues-rock prowess. Other notable albums from this period include "Watt" (1970), "A Space in Time" (1971), and "Rock & Roll Music to the World" (1972).

Alvin Lee's distinctive guitar playing and soulful vocals became synonymous with Ten Years After's sound. His technical prowess and ability to seamlessly blend blues, rock, and jazz influences made him one of the most respected guitarists of his time. The band's music often featured extended improvisations, showcasing their instrumental skills and their ability to create a mesmerizing live experience.

However, despite their musical success, internal tensions began to affect the band, and they disbanded in 1974. Alvin Lee pursued a solo career while the other members went on to various musical projects. Throughout the 1980s and 1990s, there were occasional reunions and collaborations, but it wasn't until 2002 that Ten Years After officially reformed with the original members.

Tragically, Alvin Lee passed away in 2013, leaving behind a significant legacy in the world of blues rock. Despite his absence, the surviving members, Leo Lyons, Ric Lee, and Chick Churchill, decided to continue performing under the Ten Years After name, enlisting guitarist and vocalist Marcus Bonfanti to carry on Alvin Lee's guitar-driven spirit.

Ten Years After's impact on the blues rock genre cannot be overstated. Their electrifying performances, masterful musicianship, and timeless songs continue to resonate with fans worldwide. Whether through their iconic Woodstock performance or their impressive studio albums, the band has left an indelible mark on the history of rock music, cementing their status as one of the defining acts of the late 1960s and early 1970s.

Playlist: TYA 1

"Ssssh"

With their album "Ssssh," Ten Years After cranks up the volume and unleashes a sonic storm that reverberates through the ages. Released in 1969, this album showcases the band's explosive blues-rock prowess and their ability to captivate audiences with their electrifying performances. From the infectious groove of "Bad Scene" to the searing guitar solos of "Stoned Woman," Ten Years After delivers a relentless assault of high-energy riffs and soulful vocals. "Ssssh" is a testament to the band's status as one of the pioneers of British blues rock, leaving listeners craving for more of their powerful musical sorcery.

"Goin' Home!"

Ten Years After takes listeners on a musical journey back to their roots with "Goin' Home!" This album pays homage to the band's blues influences, showcasing their ability to channel the raw emotion and gritty energy that defined the genre. From the soulful rendition of "Help Me" to the haunting beauty of "Let's Shake It Up," Ten Years After infuses their signature sound with a heartfelt authenticity that resonates deep within the soul. "Goin' Home!" is a testament to the band's reverence for the blues and their ability to reinterpret the genre with their own distinctive style.

"Cricklewood Green" (2002 Remaster)

Experience the sonic masterpiece that is "Cricklewood Green" in its remastered glory. Originally released in 1970, this album showcases Ten Years After's innovative blend of blues, rock, and jazz influences. From the infectious grooves of "Love Like a Man" to the mesmerizing guitar work of "50,000 Miles Beneath My Brain," "Cricklewood Green" immerses listeners in a world of sonic exploration and musical virtuosity. The 2002 remaster breathes new life into the album, enhancing its sonic depth and ensuring that the timeless brilliance of Ten Years After's musical prowess shines through.

"Watt"

With "Watt," Ten Years After harnesses their creative energy and delivers an album that electrifies the senses. Released in 1970, this record showcases the band's evolution as they explore new musical territories and push the boundaries of their sound. From the hard-hitting rhythms of "I'm Coming On" to the introspective beauty of "My Baby Left Me," "Watt" is a powerful testament to Ten Years After's versatility and their ability to captivate listeners with their dynamic songwriting and impassioned performances. Prepare to be engulfed in a whirlwind of musical energy that leaves you craving for more.

"Alvin Lee and Company"

"Alvin Lee and Company" is a musical journey that spotlights the extraordinary talent of Ten Years After's lead guitarist and vocalist, Alvin Lee. Released in 1972, this album showcases Lee's virtuosic guitar skills and his ability to craft memorable songs that blend elements of blues, rock, and psychedelia. From the anthemic "Keep a Knockin'" to the introspective beauty of "Lost in Love," "Alvin Lee and Company" is a testament to Lee's versatility and his ability to captivate listeners with his soulful vocals and electrifying guitar solos. Embark on a sonic adventure led by one of rock's true guitar legends.

"Undead" (Re-Presents / Live)

Relive the blistering intensity of Ten Years After's unforgettable live performance with the re-presents edition of "Undead." Originally released in 1968, this album captures the band's explosive energy and their ability to captivate audiences with their raw blues-rock power. From the frenetic guitar solos of "I Can't Keep from Crying Sometimes" to the pulsating rhythms of "Rock Your Mama," "Undead" is a sonic assault that immerses listeners in the thrilling atmosphere of a live concert experience. This re-presents edition adds an extra layer of sonic clarity and presence, allowing fans to fully appreciate the band's dynamic performance.

"The Long Road Home" (Live 1969)

Travel back in time to 1969 and join Ten Years After on "The Long Road Home," a live album that captures the band's electrifying performances from that era. This release showcases the band's raw energy and their ability to command the stage with their blues-infused rock 'n' roll.

From the epic jams of "I Can't Keep from Crying Sometimes" to the mesmerizing guitar work of "Hear Me Calling," Ten Years After takes listeners on a sonic journey that leaves them exhilarated and hungry for more. "The Long Road Home" is a testament to the band's prowess as a live act and their ability to ignite the stage with their musical fire.

"Live at the Fillmore East 1970"
Immerse yourself in the live experience of Ten Years After with "Live at the Fillmore East 1970." This album captures the band at the peak of their powers as they deliver an unforgettable performance at the historic Fillmore East. From the electrifying guitar solos of "Good Morning Little Schoolgirl" to the jam-filled frenzy of "I Can't Keep from Crying Sometimes," Ten Years After showcases their impeccable musicianship and their ability to create an atmosphere of pure rock 'n' roll ecstasy. Let the energy of the Fillmore East envelop you as you witness Ten Years After's explosive live prowess in all its glory.

- Bad Scene (2017 Remaster) 3:30   Ssssh
- Two Time Mama (2017 Remaster) 2:01   Ssssh
- Stoned Woman (2017 Remaster)   3:20   Ssssh
- Good Morning Little Schoolgirl (2017 Remaster)   7:10   Ssssh
- If You Should Love Me (2017 Remaster)   5:23   Ssssh
- I Don't Know That You Don't Know My Name (2017 Remaster)   2:05   Ssssh
- The Stomp (2017 Remaster)   4:30   Ssssh
- I Woke up This Morning (2017 Remaster) 5:32   Ssssh
- Hear Me Calling   5:43   Goin' Home!
- Going to Try   4:38   Goin' Home!
- Love Like a Man (Single Version) 3:07   Goin' Home!

- No Title   8:13   Goin' Home!
- I Woke up This Morning   5:30   Goin' Home!
- Woodchopper's Ball (Live) 7:53   Goin' Home!
- I'm Going Home (Live at Woodstock)   9:31   Goin' Home!
- Sugar the Road (2002 Remaster)   4:07   Cricklewood Green (2002 Remaster)
- Working on the Road (2002 Remaster)   4:17 Cricklewood Green (2002 Remaster)
- 50,000 Miles Beneath My Brain (2002 Remaster) 7:37 Cricklewood Green (2002 Remaster)
- Year 3,000 Blues (2002 Remaster) 2:24   Cricklewood Green (2002 Remaster)
- Me and My Baby (2002 Remaster) 4:10   Cricklewood Green (2002 Remaster)
- Love Like a Man (2002 Remaster) 7:38   Cricklewood Green (2002 Remaster)
- Circles (2002 Remaster)   3:59   Cricklewood Green (2002 Remaster)
- As the Sun Still Burns Away (2002 Remaster)   4:52 Cricklewood Green (2002 Remaster)
- Warm Sun (2002 Remaster)   3:08   Cricklewood Green (2002 Remaster)
- To No One (2002 Remaster)   3:49   Cricklewood Green (2002 Remaster)
- I'm Coming On (2017 Remaster)   3:49   Watt
- My Baby Left Me (2017 Remaster) 5:23   Watt
- Think About the Times (2017 Remaster)   4:44   Watt
- I Say Yeah (2017 Remaster) 5:18   Watt
- The Band with No Name (2017 Remaster) 1:37   Watt
- Gonna Run (2017 Remaster)   6:03   Watt
- She Lies in the Morning (2017 Remaster) 7:25   Watt
- Sweet Little Sixteen (2017 Remaster)   4:12   Watt

- The Sounds 4:13   Alvin Lee and Company
- Rock Your Mama   3:02   Alvin Lee and Company
- Hold Me Tight   2:20   Alvin Lee and Company
- Standing at the Crossroads 4:03   Alvin Lee and Company
- Portable People   2:15   Alvin Lee and Company
- Boogie On   14:31   Alvin Lee and Company
- Spider in My Web (Single Version) 7:19   Alvin Lee and Company
- Hear Me Calling (Single Version)   3:48   Alvin Lee and Company
- I'm Going Home (Single Version)   3:37   Alvin Lee and Company
- I May Be Wrong, But I Won't Be Wrong Always (Live) 10:40   Undead (Re-Presents / Live)
- (At the) Woodchopper's Ball (Live) 7:38   Undead (Re-Presents / Live)
- Spider In My Web (Live)   7:41   Undead (Re-Presents / Live)
- Summertime / Shantung Cabbage (Live)   6:05   Undead (Re-Presents / Live)
- I'm Going Home (Live)   6:25   Undead (Re-Presents / Live)
- Rock Your Mama (Live)   3:46   Undead (Re-Presents / Live)
- Spoonful (Live)   6:48   Undead (Re-Presents / Live)
- Standing At the Crossroads (Live) 5:07   Undead (Re-Presents / Live)
- I Can't Keep From Crying Sometimes / Extension On One Chord (Live)   17:07   Undead (Re-Presents / Live)
- Woman Trouble (Live At BBC "Top Gear" , London / 1968)   4:53   Undead (Re-Presents / Live)

- (At the) Woodchopper's Ball (Live At BBC "Top Gear" , London / 1968)   4:29   Undead (Re-Presents / Live)
- No Title Blues (Live At BBC "Top Gear" , London / 1968) 7:03 Undead (Re-Presents / Live)
- I'm Going Home (Live At BBC "Top Gear" , London / 1968)   4:01   Undead (Re-Presents / Live)
- Hear Me Calling (Live At BBC "David Symonds Show" , London / 1968)   4:09   Undead (Re-Presents / Live)
- Woman Trouble (Live At BBC "David Symonds Show" , London / 1968)   2:39   Undead (Re-Presents / Live)
- Standing At the Crossroads (Live At BBC "Top Gear" , London / 1968)   2:17   Undead (Re-Presents / Live)
- I May Be Wrong But I Won't Be Wrong Always (Live 1969)   9:54   The Long Road Home (Live 1969)
- Good Morning Little School Girl (Live 1969)   8:03 The Long Road Home (Live 1969)
- No Title (Live 1969)   11:36   The Long Road Home (Live 1969)
- Spider In My Web (Live 1969)   8:59   The Long Road Home (Live 1969)
- Love You Till I Die (Live 1969)   6:05   The Long Road Home (Live 1969)
- Spoonful (Live 1969)   8:07   The Long Road Home (Live 1969)
- Hobbit (Live 1969) 11:32   The Long Road Home (Live 1969)
- Scat Thing/I Can't Keep From Crying (Live 1969) 18:31 The Long Road Home (Live 1969)
- Love Like a Man (Live at the Fillmore East)   9:35 Live at the Fillmore East 1970
- Good Morning Little Schoolgirl (Live at the Fillmore East)   7:26   Live at the Fillmore East 1970

- Working on the Road (Live at the Fillmore East) 3:34
  Live at the Fillmore East 1970
- The Hobbit (Live at the Fillmore East) 10:52 Live at
  the Fillmore East 1970
- 50,000 Miles Beneath My Brain (Live at the Fillmore
  East) 9:58 Live at the Fillmore East 1970
- Skoobly - Oobly - Doobob / I Can't Keep from Crying
  Sometimes / Extension on One Chord (Live at the
  Fillmore East) 19:30 Live at the Fillmore East 1970
- Help Me (Live at the Fillmore East) 16:06 Live at the
  Fillmore East 1970
- I'm Going Home (Live at the Fillmore East) 11:57
  Live at the Fillmore East 1970
- Sweet Little Sixteen (Live at the Fillmore East) 4:38
  Live at the Fillmore East 1970
- Roll over Beethoven (Live at the Fillmore East) 4:44
  Live at the Fillmore East 1970
- I Woke up This Morning (Live at the Fillmore East)
  8:09 Live at the Fillmore East 1970
- Spoonful (Live at the Fillmore East) 8:01 Live at
  the Fillmore East 1970

Playlist: TYA 2

"A Space in Time" (Deluxe Version)
Step into a cosmic realm of sonic exploration with the Deluxe Version of Ten Years After's "A Space in Time." Originally released in 1971, this album catapults listeners into a dimension where blues, rock, and psychedelic influences intertwine. From the haunting melodies of "I'd Love to Change the World" to the mind-bending guitar work of "One of These Days," "A Space in Time" is a sonic voyage that captivates the imagination. This Deluxe Version offers a deeper dive into the album's creative process, with bonus tracks and expanded liner notes, allowing fans to fully immerse themselves in the band's interstellar musical odyssey.

"Rock & Roll Music to the World"
Ten Years After unleashes a rock 'n' roll celebration with "Rock & Roll Music to the World." Released in 1972, this album embodies the band's unabashed love for the genre, delivering a collection of hard-hitting tracks that exude pure energy. From the foot-stomping groove of the title track to

the blues-infused power of "I Woke Up This Morning," Ten Years After pays homage to the timeless spirit of rock 'n' roll. With their searing guitar solos, pulsating rhythms, and passionate vocals, the band proves once again why they are revered as one of the pioneers of British blues rock.

"Recorded Live"

Immerse yourself in the electrifying energy of a Ten Years After live performance with "Recorded Live." Released in 1973, this album captures the band's raw power and infectious stage presence, transporting listeners to the front row of a legendary concert experience. From the extended jams of "I'm Going Home" to the soulful blues of "Sweet Little Sixteen," Ten Years After showcases their improvisational prowess and their ability to captivate audiences with their dynamic musicianship. "Recorded Live" is a testament to the band's status as a powerhouse live act and a must-have for any fan seeking to relive the magic of their unforgettable performances.

"Positive Vibrations" (Deluxe Version)

Get ready for a dose of positivity and sonic bliss with the Deluxe Version of Ten Years After's "Positive Vibrations." Originally released in 1974, this album radiates with the band's infectious enthusiasm and their ability to infuse their blues-rock sound with a sunny disposition. From the uplifting vibes of "Nowhere to Run" to the anthemic energy of "Rock 'n' Roll Music to the World," "Positive Vibrations" envelops listeners in a sonic embrace that uplifts the spirit. This Deluxe Version offers additional tracks and exclusive content, allowing fans to bask in the band's positive musical journey.

"About Time"
Ten Years After proves that their musical fire still burns brightly with "About Time." Released in 1989, this album showcases the band's evolution while staying true to their blues-rock roots. From the infectious grooves of "I Get All Shook Up" to the scorching guitar solos of "I'll Make It Easy for You," "About Time" demonstrates that Ten Years After remains a force to be reckoned with. The band's seasoned musicianship and soulful delivery make this album a testament to their enduring legacy and their ability to captivate audiences across generations.

"Ten Years After"
This 2002 re-release of the eponymous album that introduced the world to Ten Years After. Originally, released in 1967, "Ten Years After" showcases the band's early blues-infused sound and sets the foundation for their future successes. From the rollicking energy of "I Want to Know" to the brooding atmosphere of "Spider in My Web," this album captures the raw power and youthful exuberance of the band's early years. With their soulful vocals, blistering guitar work, and tight-knit rhythm section, Ten Years After proves from the start that they are a force to be reckoned with in the world of blues rock.

"British Live Performance Series"
Step into the heart of a Ten Years After live performance with the "British Live Performance Series." This collection captures the band's electrifying energy and their ability to command the stage with their blues-infused rock 'n' roll. From the scorching guitar solos of "Good Morning Little Schoolgirl" to the infectious grooves of "Sweet Little Sixteen," Ten Years After delivers a live experience that is

both exhilarating and unforgettable. The "British Live Performance Series" showcases the band's unparalleled musicianship and their ability to create an atmosphere of pure rock 'n' roll ecstasy.

"Live at Anti Waa Festival 1989" (Live)
Transport yourself back to 1989 and join Ten Years After at the Anti Waa Festival for a blistering live performance. This album captures the band at the height of their powers as they deliver a setlist brimming with their classic hits and fan favorites. From the thunderous riffs of "Love Like a Man" to the soulful introspection of "I Can't Keep from Crying Sometimes," Ten Years After captivates the audience with their virtuosic musicianship and passionate delivery. "Live at Anti Waa Festival 1989" is a testament to the band's enduring legacy as a live act and their ability to ignite the stage with their rock 'n' roll magic.

"The Friday Rock Show Sessions - Live at Reading 1983"
Witness Ten Years After's explosive live energy as they take the stage at Reading in 1983 with "The Friday Rock Show Sessions." This album captures the band in peak form, delivering a high-octane performance that leaves the audience breathless. From the gritty blues-rock of "Love Like a Man" to the euphoric energy of "Good Morning Little Schoolgirl," Ten Years After showcases their impeccable musicianship and their ability to command the stage with their raw power. "The Friday Rock Show Sessions - Live at Reading 1983" is a must-have for any fan craving a taste of Ten Years After's exhilarating live experience.

"Live 1990"

Experience the vibrant energy of Ten Years After's live performance in 1990 with "Live 1990." This album captures the band's unrelenting spirit and their ability to captivate audiences with their blues-infused rock 'n' roll. From the soulful vocals of "Hear Me Calling" to the blistering guitar solos of "Good Morning Little Schoolgirl," Ten Years After showcases their enduring passion and musicianship. "Live 1990" is a testament to the band's ability to deliver a live experience that transcends time, leaving listeners craving for more of their electrifying performances

- One of These Days (2004 Remaster)   5:58   A Space in Time (Deluxe Version)
- Here They Come (2004 Remaster) 4:35   A Space in Time (Deluxe Version)
- I'd Love to Change the World (2004 Remaster)   3:44 A Space in Time (Deluxe Version)
- Over the Hill (2004 Remaster)   2:28   A Space in Time (Deluxe Version)
- Baby Won't You Let Me Rock N' Roll You (2004 Remaster)   2:14   A Space in Time (Deluxe Version)
- Once There Was a Time (2004 Remaster) 3:23   A Space in Time (Deluxe Version)
- Let the Sky Fall (2004 Remaster)   4:20   A Space in Time (Deluxe Version)
- Hard Monkeys (2004 Remaster)   3:11   A Space in Time (Deluxe Version)
- I've Been There Too (2004 Remaster)   5:45   A Space in Time (Deluxe Version)
- Uncle Jam (2004 Remaster) 2:00   A Space in Time (Deluxe Version)
- One of These Days (Stereo Quad Mix)   5:56   A Space in Time (Deluxe Version)

- Here They Come (Stereo Quad Mix) 4:36 A Space in Time (Deluxe Version)
- I'd Love to Change the World (Stereo Quad Mix) 3:43 A Space in Time (Deluxe Version)
- Over the Hill (Stereo Quad Mix) 2:29 A Space in Time (Deluxe Version)
- Baby Won't You Let Me Rock N' Roll You (Stereo Quad Mix) 2:19 A Space in Time (Deluxe Version)
- Once There Was a Time (Stereo Quad Mix) 3:26 A Space in Time (Deluxe Version)
- Let the Sky Fall (Stereo Quad Mix) 4:19 A Space in Time (Deluxe Version)
- Hard Monkeys (Stereo Quad Mix) 3:13 A Space in Time (Deluxe Version)
- I've Been There Too (Stereo Quad Mix) 5:49 A Space in Time (Deluxe Version)
- Uncle Jam (Stereo Quad Mix) 1:55 A Space in Time (Deluxe Version)
- You Give Me Loving 6:31 Rock & Roll Music to the World
- Convention Prevention 4:22 Rock & Roll Music to the World
- Turned off Tv Blues 5:12 Rock & Roll Music to the World
- Standing at the Station 7:08 Rock & Roll Music to the World
- You Can't Win Them All 4:05 Rock & Roll Music to the World
- Religion 5:50 Rock & Roll Music to the World
- Choo Choo Mama 4:02 Rock & Roll Music to the World
- Tomorrow I'll Be out of Town 4:26 Rock & Roll Music to the World

- Rock & Roll Music to the World   3:49   Rock & Roll Music to the World
- One of These Days (Live in Frankfurt)   6:29 Recorded Live
- You Give Me Loving (Live in Frankfurt)   6:02 Recorded Live
- Good Morning Little Schoolgirl (Live in Frankfurt) 7:26 Recorded Live
- The Hobbit (Live in Frankfurt)   8:35   Recorded Live
- Help Me (Live in Amsterdam)   11:02   Recorded Live
- Time Is Flying (Live in Frankfurt) 5:36   Recorded Live
- Standing at the Station (Live in Frankfurt) 11:50 Recorded Live
- Jam (Live in Amsterdam)   18:08   Recorded Live
- Help Me (Live in Paris)   12:07   Recorded Live
- I Woke up This Morning (Live in Rotterdam)   4:26 Recorded Live
- Sweet Little Sixteen (Live in Frankfurt)   4:24 Recorded Live
- Jam (Live in Frankfurt)   16:31   Recorded Live
- Classical Thing (Live in Paris)   0:54   Recorded Live
- Scat Thing (Live in Paris)   0:57   Recorded Live
- I Can't Keep from Crying Sometimes, Pt. 1 (Live in Paris) 1:57 Recorded Live
- Extension on One Chord (Live in Paris)   10:45 Recorded Live
- I Can't Keep from Crying Sometimes, Pt. 2 (Live in Paris) 3:12 Recorded Live
- Silly Thing (Live in Frankfurt)   1:08   Recorded Live
- Slow Blues in C (Live in Frankfurt) 8:14   Recorded Live
- I'm Going Home (Live in Frankfurt)   10:54 Recorded Live

- Choo Choo Mama (Live in Frankfurt)   3:21
  Recorded Live
- Nowhere to Run (2013 Remaster) 4:01   Positive
  Vibrations (Deluxe Version)
- Positive Vibrations (2013 Remaster)   4:17
  Positive Vibrations (Deluxe Version)
- Stone Me (2013 Remaster) 4:55   Positive Vibrations
  (Deluxe Version)
- Without You (2013 Remaster)   3:58   Positive
  Vibrations (Deluxe Version)
- Going Back to Birmingham (2013 Remaster)   2:38
  Positive Vibrations (Deluxe Version)
- It's Getting Harder (2013 Remaster)   4:23
  Positive Vibrations (Deluxe Version)
- You're Driving Me Crazy (2013 Remaster) 2:24
  Positive Vibrations (Deluxe Version)
- Look into My Life (2013 Remaster) 4:15   Positive
  Vibrations (Deluxe Version)
- Look Me Straight into the Eyes (2013 Remaster)   6:18
  Positive Vibrations (Deluxe Version)
- I Wanted to Boogie (2013 Remaster)   3:35
  Positive Vibrations (Deluxe Version)
- Rock & Roll Music to the World (Live in Frankfurt)
  4:22 Positive Vibrations (Deluxe Version)
- Once There Was a Time (Live in Frankfurt)   3:21
  Positive Vibrations (Deluxe Version)
- Spoonful (Live in Paris)   6:24   Positive Vibrations
  (Deluxe Version)
- I'm Going Home (Live in Paris)   11:35   Positive
  Vibrations (Deluxe Version)
- Standing at the Station (Live in Amsterdam)   11:00
  Positive Vibrations (Deluxe Version)

- Sweet Little Sixteen (Live in Atlanta)   4:50
  Positive Vibrations (Deluxe Version)
- Positive Vibrations Radio Advert (1974)   0:36
  Positive Vibrations (Deluxe Version)
- Highway of Love   5:12   About Time
- Let's Shake It Up   5:22   About Time
- I Get All Shook Up 4:41   About Time
- Victim of Circumstance   4:32   About Time
- Going to Chicago   4:27   About Time
- Saturday Night   4:08   About Time
- Bad Blood   7:13   About Time
- Working in a Parking Lot 4:56   About Time
- Wild Is the River   3:57   About Time
- Outside My Window   5:48   About Time
- Waiting for the Judgement Day   4:33   About Time
- I Want to Know   2:10   Ten Years After
- I Can't Keep from Crying, Sometimes   5:22   Ten Years After
- Adventures of a Young Organ   2:33   Ten Years After
- Spoonful   6:03   Ten Years After
- Losing the Dogs   3:01   Ten Years After
- Feel It for Me   2:39   Ten Years After
- Love Until I Die   2:04   Ten Years After
- Don't Want You Woman   2:35   Ten Years After
- Help Me   9:49   Ten Years After
- Portable People (Mono Single Version)   2:15   Ten Years After
- The Sounds (Mono Single Version) 4:27   Ten Years After
- Rock Your Mama   2:58   Ten Years After
- Spider In My Web (Single Version) 7:08   Ten Years After

- Hold Me Tight   2:16   Ten Years After
- At the Woodchoppers Ball (Live "Undead" Version)
  7:44 Ten Years After
- Let's Shake It Up (Live)   3:43   British Live
  Performance Series
- Good Morning Little Schoolgirl (Live)   6:49   British
  Live Performance Series
- Slow Blues in C (Live)   5:56   British Live
  Performance Series
- Hobbit (Live)   2:35   British Live Performance
  Series
- Love Like a Man (Live)   5:04   British Live
  Performance Series
- Johnny B. Goode (Live)   1:34   British Live
  Performance Series
- Bad Blood (Live)   5:55   British Live Performance
  Series
- Victim of Circumstance (Live)   4:09   British Live
  Performance Series
- I Can't Keep from Crying Sometimes (Live)   10:35
  British Live Performance Series
- I'm Going Home (Live)   9:52   British Live
  Performance Series
- Sweet Little Sixteen (Live) 4:07   British Live
  Performance Series
- Introduction (Live) 0:14   Live at Anti Waa Festival 1989
  (Live)
- Rock 'n' Roll Music to the World (Live)   4:00   Live at
  Anti Waa Festival 1989 (Live)
- Hear Me Calling (Live)   4:25   Live at Anti Waa
  Festival 1989 (Live)
- Good Morning Little Schoolgirl (Live)   6:49   Live at
  Anti Waa Festival 1989 (Live)

- Slow Blues in C (Live)   6:16   Live at Anti Waa Festival 1989 (Live)
- Victim of Circumstance (Live)   4:29   Live at Anti Waa Festival 1989 (Live)
- Drumsolo Ric Lee (Live)   6:55   Live at Anti Waa Festival 1989 (Live)
- Love Like a Man (Live)   5:32   Live at Anti Waa Festival 1989 (Live)
- Johnny B. Goode (Live)   2:00   Live at Anti Waa Festival 1989 (Live)
- Help Me (Live)   9:02   Live at Anti Waa Festival 1989 (Live)
- I'm Going Home (Live)   12:14   Live at Anti Waa Festival 1989 (Live)
- Choo Choo Mama (Live)   3:23   Live at Anti Waa Festival 1989 (Live)
- Sweet Little Sixteen (Live) 4:15   Live at Anti Waa Festival 1989 (Live)
- Love Like a Man (Live)   5:12   The Friday Rock Show Sessions - Live at Reading 1983
- Good Morning Little Schoolgirl (Live)   6:28   The Friday Rock Show Sessions - Live at Reading 1983
- Slow Blues in 'C' (Live)   5:49   The Friday Rock Show Sessions - Live at Reading 1983
- Suzie Q (Live)   7:03   The Friday Rock Show Sessions - Live at Reading 1983
- Hobbit (Live)   4:12   The Friday Rock Show Sessions - Live at Reading 1983
- I May Be Wrong but I Won't Be Wrong Always (Live)   6:02 The Friday Rock Show Sessions - Live at Reading 1983

- I Can't Keep from Cryin' Sometimes/Extension on One Chord (Live)   9:29   The Friday Rock Show Sessions - Live at Reading 1983
- Going Home (Live) 9:51   The Friday Rock Show Sessions - Live at Reading 1983
- Let's Shake It Up (Live)   3:44   Live 1990
- Good Morning Little Schoolgirl (Live)   6:50   Live 1990
- Slow Blues In C (Live)   5:48   Live 1990
- Hobbit (Live)   2:45   Live 1990
- Love Like a Man (Live)   5:05   Live 1990
- Johnny B. Goode (Live)   1:34   Live 1990
- Bad Blood (Live)   5:56   Live 1990
- Victim of Circumstance (Live)   4:08   Live 1990
- I Can't Keep from Crying (Live)   10:34   Live 1990
- I'm Goin' Home (Live)   9:48   Live 1990
- Sweet Little Sixteen (Live)   4:57   Live 1990

Playlist: TYA 3

"Evolution"

"Evolution" marks a new chapter in Ten Years After's musical journey following the departure of lead guitarist Alvin Lee. Released in 2008, this album showcases the band's ability to evolve and adapt while staying true to their blues-rock roots. With new guitarist Joe Gooch stepping into the spotlight, Ten Years After delivers a collection of soulful tracks that blend intricate guitar work, infectious rhythms, and heartfelt vocals. From the captivating melodies of "Nowhere to Run" to the introspective beauty of "I'll Make It Easy for You," "Evolution" proves that the band's spirit and musicianship remain as powerful as ever.

"A Sting in the Tale"

With "A Sting in the Tale," Ten Years After unleashes a sonic adventure that reaffirms their status as masters of blues-infused rock. Released in 2017, this album showcases the band's ability to create music that is both timeless and relevant. From the rollicking energy of "Land of the Vandals" to the introspective introspection of "Suranne Suranne," Ten Years After proves that their creative fire continues to burn brightly. With soulful vocals, fiery guitar solos, and a rhythm section that drives the music forward, "A Sting in the Tale" is a testament to the band's enduring legacy and their ability to captivate audiences with their electrifying sound.

"Naturally Live"
Experience the raw energy and unfiltered intensity of a Ten Years After live performance with "Naturally Live." This album captures the band in their element, delivering an electrifying setlist that spans their illustrious career. From the bluesy grooves of "Love Like a Man" to the epic jams of "I'm Going Home," Ten Years After showcases their unmatched musicianship and their ability to captivate audiences with their dynamic live show. "Naturally Live" is a testament to the band's dedication to their craft and their unwavering commitment to delivering a memorable live experience.

"British Live Performance Series"
Immerse yourself in the vibrant live energy of Ten Years After with the "British Live Performance Series." This collection captures the band's electrifying live performances, showcasing their timeless blend of blues and rock 'n' roll. From the scorching guitar solos of "I Can't Keep from Crying Sometimes" to the infectious groove of "Sweet Little Sixteen," Ten Years After demonstrates their mastery of the stage and their ability to captivate audiences with their unrivaled musicianship. The "British Live Performance Series" is a testament to the band's enduring legacy and their status as one of the finest live acts in rock history.

"The Name Remains the Same" (Live)
Ten Years After continues their legacy with "The Name
Remains the Same," a powerful live album that showcases the
band's unrelenting passion for blues-infused rock. Recorded
during their electrifying performances, this album captures
the energy and intensity that has become synonymous with
Ten Years After's name. From the blistering guitar solos of
"One of These Days" to the soulful vocals of "I Can't Keep
from Crying Sometimes," the band proves that their spirit
and musicianship remain as vibrant as ever. "The Name
Remains the Same" is a testament to Ten Years After's ability
to captivate audiences and keep the flame of their legacy
burning bright.

"Get the Gringo" (Original Motion Picture Soundtrack)
Ten Years After contributed the song "50,000 Miles Beneath
My Brain" to the "Get the Gringo" soundtrack. As the closing
track of the album, this epic 7-minute and 38-second journey
showcases the band's mastery of their instruments and their
ability to craft a captivating musical experience. With its
mesmerizing guitar solos, pulsating rhythms, and soulful
vocals, "50,000 Miles Beneath My Brain" immerses listeners
in a sonic landscape that perfectly complements the intensity
and atmosphere of the film. It serves as a testament to Ten
Years After's enduring musical prowess and their ability to
create music that leaves a lasting impression.

- I Think It's Gonna Rain All Night 4:27   Evolution
- She Keeps Walking 5:53   Evolution
- Why'd They Call It Falling 6:29   Evolution
- She Needed a Rock 4:31   Evolution
- My Imagination   5:14   Evolution
- I Never Saw It Coming   6:09   Evolution

- Slip Slide Away   4:36   Evolution
- Tail Lights   4:35   Evolution
- Angry Words   8:24   Evolution
- That's Alright   5:02   Evolution
- Land of the Vandals 4:09   A Sting in the Tale
- Iron Horse   3:25   A Sting in the Tale
- Miss Constable   4:06   A Sting in the Tale
- Up in Smoke   6:13   A Sting in the Tale
- Retired Hurt   5:35   A Sting in the Tale
- Suranne Suranne   3:23   A Sting in the Tale
- Stoned Alone   4:08   A Sting in the Tale
- Two Lost Souls   4:06   A Sting in the Tale
- Diamond Girl   5:16   A Sting in the Tale
- Last Night of the Bottle   4:08   A Sting in the Tale
- Guitar Hero 4:55   A Sting in the Tale
- Silverspoon Lady   3:18   A Sting in the Tale
- Land of the Vandals (Live) 3:46   Naturally Live
- One of These Days (Live) 5:08   Naturally Live
- Hear Me Calling (Live)   6:28   Naturally Live
- I'd Love to Change the World (Live)   6:36
  Naturally Live
- Silverspoon Lady (Live)   4:15   Naturally Live
- Last Night of the Bottle (Live)   5:50   Naturally Live
- Portable People (Live)   3:01   Naturally Live
- Don't Want You Woman (Live)   4:03   Naturally Live
- Losing the Dogs (Live)   3:35   Naturally Live
- 50,000 Miles Beneath My Brain (Live)   7:39
  Naturally Live
- Good Morning Little Schoolgirl (Live)   7:52
  Naturally Live
- I'm Going Home (Live)   10:36   Naturally Live
- Ric Lee Introducing Tya (Live)   2:29   Naturally Live

- Let's Shake It Up (Live)   3:43   British Live Performance Series
- Good Morning Little Schoolgirl (Live)   6:49   British Live Performance Series
- Slow Blues in C (Live)   5:56   British Live Performance Series
- Hobbit (Live)   2:35 · British Live Performance Series
- Love Like a Man (Live)   5:04   British Live Performance Series
- Johnny B. Goode (Live)   1:34   British Live Performance Series
- Bad Blood (Live)   5:55   British Live Performance Series
- Victim of Circumstance (Live)   4:09   British Live Performance Series
- I Can't Keep from Crying Sometimes (Live)   10:35   British Live Performance Series
- I'm Going Home (Live)   9:52   British Live Performance Series
- Sweet Little Sixteen (Live)   4:07   British Live Performance Series
- Speed Kills   3:40   Stonedhenge
- Sugar the Road (Live)   4:31   The Name Remains the Same (Live)
- One of These Days (Live)   5:37   The Name Remains the Same (Live)
- I'm Coming On (Live)   4:26   The Name Remains the Same (Live)
- Nowhere to Run (Live)   4:18   The Name Remains the Same (Live)
- Me & My Baby (Live)   4:49   The Name Remains the Same (Live)

- Standing at the Station (Live)   8:04   The Name Remains the Same (Live)
- I Say Yeah (Live)   4:00   The Name Remains the Same (Live)
- Good Morning Little Schoolgirl (Live)   8:07   The Name Remains the Same (Live)
- Help Me Baby (Live)   10:13   The Name Remains the Same (Live)
- I'm Going Home (Live)   8:36   The Name Remains the Same (Live)
- Choo Choo Mama (Live)   3:47   The Name Remains the Same (Live)
- Love Like a Man, Pt. 1 / Love Jam Two / Love Like a Man, Pt. 2 (Bonus Medley Track) [Live]   7:30   The Name Remains the Same (Live)
- 50,000 miles Beneath My Brain   7:38   Get the Gringo (Original Motion Picture Soundtrack)

Playlist: Alvin Lee

"Pump Iron"
Alvin Lee pumps up the volume and delivers a high-octane rock experience with "Pump Iron." Released in 1975, this solo album showcases Lee's electrifying guitar skills and soulful vocals. From the adrenaline-fueled title track to the bluesy swagger of "Take the Money," Lee's unmistakable talent and energy shine through. With its driving rhythms, infectious hooks, and Lee's virtuosic fretwork, "Pump Iron" is a testament to his status as a rock icon and a must-have for any fan of his electrifying style.

"Rocket Fuel"
Prepare for a sonic blast-off with Alvin Lee's "Rocket Fuel." Released in 1978, this album ignites the speakers with its explosive mix of blues, rock, and Lee's signature guitar wizardry. From the infectious groove of the title track to the fiery solos of "Let Me Be Your Loving Man," "Rocket Fuel" propels listeners on a high-energy musical journey. Lee's soulful vocals and dynamic songwriting showcase his

versatility as an artist, making this album a standout in his solo discography.

"Let It Rock"
Alvin Lee cranks up the volume and lets the music do the talking on "Let It Rock." Released in 1978, this album captures Lee's raw rock 'n' roll spirit and showcases his exceptional guitar skills. From the foot-stomping energy of the title track to the bluesy introspection of "Lonely Nights," Lee's passionate delivery and electrifying solos captivate the listener. "Let It Rock" is a testament to Lee's ability to blend blues, rock, and soul into a cohesive and powerful musical statement.

"Rx5"
Alvin Lee embraces a more experimental sound with "Rx5." Released in 1981, this album showcases Lee's willingness to push musical boundaries and venture into new sonic territories. From the synth-driven grooves of "Double Loser" to the infectious hooks of "It Ain't Easy," "Rx5" offers a unique blend of rock, pop, and electronic elements. Lee's soulful vocals and inventive guitar work shine throughout, making this album a fascinating and intriguing chapter in his solo career.

"Detroit Diesel"
Alvin Lee takes listeners on a high-octane journey with "Detroit Diesel." Released in 1986, this album captures the raw power and energy of Lee's blues-rock roots. From the driving riffs of the title track to the soulful introspection of "Gonna Turn You On," "Detroit Diesel" showcases Lee's virtuosity as a guitarist and his ability to infuse his music with gritty emotion. With its powerhouse performances and

infectious melodies, this album reaffirms Lee's status as a
legendary figure in the world of rock.

"Zoom"
Alvin Lee invites listeners to "Zoom" into a world of
infectious grooves and soaring guitar solos. Released in 1992,
this album finds Lee embracing a contemporary sound while
staying true to his blues-rock roots. From the funky rhythms
of "Real Life Blues" to the melodic hooks of "Wake Up
Moma," "Zoom" showcases Lee's ability to craft catchy,
guitar-driven rock songs. With his passionate vocals and
impeccable musicianship, Lee proves that he remains a force
to be reckoned with in the ever-evolving rock landscape.

"In Tennessee" (Deluxe Version)
Experience Alvin Lee's musical homage to the heartland of
American blues with the Deluxe Version of "In Tennessee."
Originally released in 2004, this album takes listeners on a
soul-stirring journey through Lee's interpretations of classic
blues songs. From the heartfelt rendition of "Lost in Love" to
the foot-stomping energy of "I Don't Give a Damn," Lee's
love and respect for the blues shine through. The Deluxe
Version includes bonus tracks and enhanced content that
provides a deeper dive into Lee's connection to the music
that influenced him.

"Saguitar"
Alvin Lee showcases his guitar prowess and musical
versatility on "Saguitar." Released in 2007, this instrumental
album allows Lee's guitar to take center stage as he weaves
intricate melodies, blistering solos, and soulful
improvisations. From the bluesy swagger of "The Slightest
Distance" to the jazz-infused "Blue and Blue," "Saguitar" is a

masterclass in guitar virtuosity. Lee's technical mastery and emotional depth shine through, creating a mesmerizing listening experience for guitar enthusiasts and music lovers alike.

"The Last Show"
"The Last Show" immortalizes Alvin Lee's final live performance recorded in 2012. This album captures the magic and energy of Lee's onstage presence as he delivers a career-spanning setlist that showcases his iconic guitar skills and powerful vocals. From the explosive rendition of "I'm Going Home" to the soulful rendition of "I Can't Keep from Crying Sometimes," Lee's performance is a testament to his enduring talent and his status as a rock legend. "The Last Show" serves as a fitting tribute to a remarkable artist and a must-have for fans of Lee's unparalleled stage presence.

"Alvin Lee & Co." (Live at the Academy of Music, New York, 1975)
Immerse yourself in the electrifying energy of Alvin Lee's live performance with "Alvin Lee & Co." This album captures the raw power and virtuosity of Lee's guitar playing, backed by a stellar band, as they take the stage at the Academy of Music in New York in 1975. From the blistering solos of "Keep On Rockin'" to the bluesy grooves of "Slow Blues in C," Lee and his band deliver a mesmerizing set that showcases their undeniable chemistry and musicianship. "Alvin Lee & Co." is a testament to Lee's ability to captivate audiences with his dynamic stage presence and undeniable talent.

"Live at Rockpalast" (Remastered)
Relive the exhilaration of Alvin Lee's captivating live performance with the remastered edition of "Live at Rockpalast." This album captures Lee's explosive energy and magnetic stage presence as he commands the stage with his unparalleled guitar skills. Recorded in 1978, this remastered edition breathes new life into the iconic performance, allowing fans to experience the raw power and infectious grooves of songs like "I Want You (She's So Heavy)" and "Choo Choo Mama" in pristine audio quality. "Live at Rockpalast" is a testament to Lee's status as a dynamic live performer and a must-have for any fan of his legendary talent.

"Live In Vienna"
Alvin Lee brings his energetic live show to Vienna with "Live In Vienna." This album captures the magic and excitement of Lee's performance as he delivers a blistering set of blues-infused rock 'n' roll. From the fiery guitar solos of "Gonna Turn You On" to the anthemic sing-alongs of "Hey Joe," Lee and his band create an electrifying atmosphere that leaves the audience in awe. "Live In Vienna" is a testament to Lee's ability to connect with his fans through his dynamic stage presence and his unmatched musicianship.

"Ride On"
"Ride On" takes listeners on a sonic journey through Alvin Lee's musical landscape. Released in 2012, this album showcases Lee's versatility as a songwriter and his ability to blend genres seamlessly. From the infectious blues-rock of "Love Like a Man" to the introspective balladry of "Lost in Love," "Ride On" encapsulates Lee's unique musical vision. With his soulful vocals, emotive guitar playing, and

captivating songwriting, Lee reminds us why he remains a beloved figure in the world of rock.

"Keep on Rockin'"
Alvin Lee keeps the rock 'n' roll spirit alive and kicking with "Keep on Rockin'." Released in 2013, this album showcases Lee's timeless sound and infectious energy. From the foot-stomping rhythm of the title track to the bluesy charm of "Rock 'n' Roll Guitar Picker," Lee's passion and love for music shine through. With its catchy hooks, energetic performances, and Lee's signature guitar work, "Keep on Rockin'" is a celebration of the enduring power of rock 'n' roll and a fitting testament to Lee's incredible musical legacy.

- One More Chance 3:54   Pump Iron
- Try to Be Righteous 4:04   Pump Iron
- You Told Me   3:53   Pump Iron
- Have Mercy 2:49   Pump Iron
- Julian Rice 4:55   Pump Iron
- Time and Space   2:43   Pump Iron
- Burnt Fungus   3:16   Pump Iron
- The Darkest Night 2:26   Pump Iron
- It's All Right Now 2:39   Pump Iron
- Truckin Down the Other Way   2:31   Pump Iron
- Let the Sea Burn Down   6:46   Pump Iron
- Madness   1:52   Pump Iron
- Midnight Special   4:51   Pump Iron
- Rocket Fuel 3:18   Rocket Fuel
- Gonna Turn You On   4:59   Rocket Fuel
- Friday the 13th   4:56   Rocket Fuel
- Somebody Callin' Me   5:56   Rocket Fuel
- Ain't Nothin' Shakin'   5:02   Rocket Fuel
- Alvin's Blue Thing 0:27   Rocket Fuel

- Baby Don't You Cry 3:16   Rocket Fuel
- The Devil's Screaming   9:44   Rocket Fuel
- Chemicals, Chemistry, Mystery & More   3:52   Let It Rock
- Love the Way You Rock Me   3:19   Let It Rock
- Ain't Nobody   5:08   Let It Rock
- Images Shifting   4:45   Let It Rock
- Little Boy   4:45   Let It Rock
- Downhill Lady Racer   3:42   Let It Rock
- World Is Spinning Faster   5:27   Let It Rock
- Through with Your Lovin'   5:00   Let It Rock
- Time to Meditate   3:56   Let It Rock
- Let It Rock   3:00   Let It Rock
- Snake Jam   4:51   Let It Rock
- Break Jam   6:51   Let It Rock
- Hang On   3:47   Rx5
- Lady Luck   3:05   Rx5
- Can't Stop   5:09   Rx5
- Wrong Side of the Law   3:14   Rx5
- Nutbush City Limits   3:53   Rx5
- Rock-N Roll Guitar Picker   3:06   Rx5
- Double Loser   2:54   Rx5
- Fool No More   5:22   Rx5
- Dangerous World   3:45   Rx5
- High Times 5:33   Rx5
- Shuffle It (Bonus Track)   6:10   Rx5
- Detroit Diesel   4:41   Detroit Diesel
- Shot in the Dark   4:07   Detroit Diesel
- Too Late to Run for Cover   3:50   Detroit Diesel
- Talk Don't Bother Me   3:40   Detroit Diesel
- Ordinary Man   4:04   Detroit Diesel
- Heart of Stone   4:07   Detroit Diesel
- She's so Cute   3:18   Detroit Diesel

- Back in My Arms Again   3:47   Detroit Diesel
- Don't Want to Fight   4:31   Detroit Diesel
- Let's Go   3:27   Detroit Diesel
- A Little Bit of Love 3:56   Zoom
- Real Life Blues   4:35   Zoom
- The Price of This Love   4:07   Zoom
- Moving the Blues   4:04   Zoom
- Lost in Love   4:08   Zoom
- Wake up Moma   3:59   Zoom
- It Dont Come Easy 5:08   Zoom
- Rememebr Me   4:39   Zoom
- Anything for You   4:59   Zoom
- Jenny Jenny 4:25   Zoom
- Use That Power   4:20   Zoom
- Let's Boogie 3:34   In Tennessee (Deluxe Version)
- Rock & Roll Girls   3:38   In Tennessee (Deluxe Version)
- Take My Time   4:45   In Tennessee (Deluxe Version)
- I'm Gonna Make It 6:10   In Tennessee (Deluxe Version)
- Something's Gonna Get You   4:47   In Tennessee (Deluxe Version)
- Why Did You Do It 4:48   In Tennessee (Deluxe Version)
- Getting Nowhere Fast   4:41   In Tennessee (Deluxe Version)
- How Do You Do It 5:01   In Tennessee (Deluxe Version)
- Let's Get It On   5:26   In Tennessee (Deluxe Version)
- Tell Me Why   5:53   In Tennessee (Deluxe Version)
- I'm Going Home   6:13   In Tennessee (Deluxe Version)
- Mystery Train (Live)   4:18   In Tennessee (Deluxe Version)
- Don't Be Cruel (Live)   2:39   In Tennessee (Deluxe Version)
- Money Honey (Live)   3:02   In Tennessee (Deluxe Version)

- My Baby Left Me (Live)   2:12   In Tennessee (Deluxe Version)
- Rip It up (Live)   3:43   In Tennessee (Deluxe Version)
- Anytime U Want Me   4:52   Saguitar
- The Squeeze   4:08   Saguitar
- It's Time to Play   4:24   Saguitar
- Midnite Train   2:20   Saguitar
- Motel Blues 5:21   Saguitar
- Only Here for the Ride   2:48   Saguitar
- Memphis   2:03   Saguitar
- Got a Lot of Living to Do   3:07   Saguitar
- Blues Has Got a Hold On Me   3:26   Saguitar
- It's All Good   4:21   Saguitar
- Education   4:31   Saguitar
- Rapper   3:29   Saguitar
- Smoking Rope   4:40   Saguitar
- Rocking Rendezvous   4:40   Saguitar
- Hear Me Calling   5:22   The Last Show
- I Can't Keep from Crying Sometimes   11:03   The Last Show
- How Do You Do It   4:31   The Last Show
- My Baby Left Me   2:13   The Last Show
- Country Thing   0:48   The Last Show
- I Don't Give a Damn   5:02   The Last Show
- I'm Writing You a Letter   7:50   The Last Show
- Slow Blues in 'C'   8:19   The Last Show
- I'm Gonna Make It 5:11   The Last Show
- Scat Encounter   0:48   The Last Show
- I Woke up This Morning   5:04   The Last Show
- Love Like a Man   8:09   The Last Show
- Going Home   11:34   The Last Show
- Rip It Up   3:05   The Last Show

- Got to Keep Moving (Live) 5:59   Alvin Lee & Co. (Live at the Academy of Music, New York, 1975)
- Let's Get Back (Live)   8:37   Alvin Lee & Co. (Live at the Academy of Music, New York, 1975)
- Somebody Callin' Me (Live)   6:30   Alvin Lee & Co. (Live at the Academy of Music, New York, 1975)
- All Life's Trials (Live)   2:50   Alvin Lee & Co. (Live at the Academy of Music, New York, 1975)
- Baby Please Don't Go (Live)   2:09   Alvin Lee & Co. (Live at the Academy of Music, New York, 1975)
- Time and Space (Live)   2:45   Alvin Lee & Co. (Live at the Academy of Music, New York, 1975)
- There's a Feeling (Live)   4:46   Alvin Lee & Co. (Live at the Academy of Music, New York, 1975)
- Every Blues You've Ever Heard (Live)   5:37   Alvin Lee & Co. (Live at the Academy of Music, New York, 1975)
- Percy's Roots (Live) 17:32   Alvin Lee & Co. (Live at the Academy of Music, New York, 1975)
- Money Honey (Live)   2:58   Alvin Lee & Co. (Live at the Academy of Music, New York, 1975)
- Going Through the Door (Live)   6:03   Alvin Lee & Co. (Live at the Academy of Music, New York, 1975)
- I'm Writing You a Letter (Live)   6:27   Alvin Lee & Co. (Live at the Academy of Music, New York, 1975)
- Ride My Train (Live)   15:46   Alvin Lee & Co. (Live at the Academy of Music, New York, 1975)
- Gonna Turn You On (Live) [Remastered]   4:23   Live at Rockpalast (Remastered)
- Help Me (Live) [Remastered]   8:47   Live at Rockpalast (Remastered)
- Ain't Nothing Shakin' (Live) [Remastered]   14:45   Live at Rockpalast (Remastered)

- Just Another Boogie (Live) [Remastered] 7:11 Live at Rockpalast (Remastered)
- Hey Joe (Live) [Remastered] 7:18 Live at Rockpalast (Remastered)
- I'm Going Home (Live) [Remastered] 9:35 Live at Rockpalast (Remastered)
- Choo Choo Moma (Live) [Remastered] 1:54 Live at Rockpalast (Remastered)
- Rip It Up (Live) [Remastered] 2:28 Live at Rockpalast (Remastered)
- Sweet Little Sixteen (Live) [Remastered] 3:37 Live at Rockpalast (Remastered)
- Roll over Beethoven (Live) [Remastered] 3:24 Live at Rockpalast (Remastered)
- Keep On Rockin' 4:15 Live In Vienna
- Long Legs 8:18 Live In Vienna
- I Hear You Knockin' 3:37 Live In Vienna
- Hear Me Calling 5:29 Live In Vienna
- Love Like a Man 5:33 Live In Vienna
- Jonny B Goode 2:00 Live In Vienna
- I Don't Give a Damn 5:32 Live In Vienna
- Good Morning Little Schoolgirl 7:42 Live In Vienna
- Skooboly Oobly Doobob 1:12 Live In Vienna
- Help Me Baby 9:49 Live In Vienna
- Classical Thing 0:56 Live In Vienna
- Going Home 13:25 Live In Vienna
- Rip It Up 3:44 Live In Vienna
- Ain't Nothin' Shakin' (Live) 5:32 Ride On
- Scat Encounter (Live) 0:58 Ride On
- Hey Joe (Live) 5:59 Ride On
- Going Home (Live) 8:48 Ride On
- Too Much 3:53 Ride On
- It's a Gaz 4:03 Ride On

- Ride on Cowboy   3:14   Ride On
- Sittin' Here 4:00   Ride On
- Can't Sleep at Night 2:31   Ride On
- Keep on Rockin'   5:08   Keep on Rockin'
- Long Legs   6:16   Keep on Rockin'
- I Hear You Knockin'   3:40   Keep on Rockin'
- Ain't Nobody's Business   4:11   Keep on Rockin'
- The Bluest Blues   7:27   Keep on Rockin'
- Boogie All Day   3:53   Keep on Rockin'
- My Baby's Come Back to Me   4:58   Keep on Rockin'
- Take It Easy 6:25   Keep on Rockin'
- Play It Like It Used to Be   4:02   Keep on Rockin'
- Give Me Your Love 5:59   Keep on Rockin'
- I Don't Give a Damn   5:47   Keep on Rockin'
- I Want You (She's so Heavy)   9:51   Keep on Rockin'
- A Little Bit of Love 3:55   Keep on Rockin'
- Real Life Blues   4:35   Keep on Rockin'
- The Price of This Love   4:07   Keep on Rockin'
- Moving the Blues   4:04   Keep on Rockin'
- Lost in Love   4:07   Keep on Rockin'
- Wake up Moma   3:58   Keep on Rockin'
- It Don't Come Easy 5:07   Keep on Rockin'
- Remember Me   4:38   Keep on Rockin'
- Anything for You   5:00   Keep on Rockin'
- Jenny, Jenny 4:25   Keep on Rockin'
- Use That Power   4:22   Keep on Rockin'
- Private Movie (feat. Alvin Lee)   3:16   Private Movie (feat. Alvin Lee) - Single
- Wishing Well (feat. Alvin Lee & Tom Compton)   3:39   Wishing Well (feat. Alvin Lee & Tom Compton) - Single

Resources

Apple Music Guide
https://support.apple.com/guide/music-web/welcome/web

Apple Music: Our Complete Guide
https://www.macrumors.com/guide/apple-music/

Apple Music basics: How to get started, make playlists, and more
https://appleinsider.com/inside/apple-music/tips/apple-music-basics-how-to-get-started-make-playlists-and-more

How to create and share a playlist in Apple Music on iPhone, iPad, and iPod touch — Apple Support
https://www.youtube.com/watch?v=c6wRCTPD8M4

Using Apple Music Playlists: How to Get Started
https://www.makeuseof.com/tag/apple-music-playlists-guide/

How to Create an Apple Music Playlist on iPhone, iPad and Mac
https://macreports.com/how-to-create-an-apple-music-playlist-on-iphone-ipad-and-mac/

Upcoming Apple Music Companions

David Bowie - Rickie Lee Jones - Protest Songs
Bob Dylan - The Doors - British Blues Rock Volume 2
The Who - Santana - CSN&Y

Printed in Great Britain
by Amazon

36637441R00086